'As a redund[...] an ending – [...] can be the best kind of beginning. Packed full of realistic inspiration, advice and motivation, this is the perfect guidebook for the moment when your career punches you in the face'
Viv Groskop, author of *Lift As You Climb: Women and the Art of Ambition*

'Eleanor Tweddell has created a book that is part-survival guide, part-life coach. This book will help you escape the valleys of rejection, bound for the peaks of opportunity'
Bruce Daisley, bestselling author of *The Joy of Work*

'This book is so much more than a user guide to life after redundancy – it's an inspiring lesson in how to deal with the knocks of everyday life, written with humour, empathy and honesty'
Debbie Hewitt, MBE, Chair, Visa Europe

'A sensitive balance of acknowledging the seriousness of redundancy by providing practical, real-world advice for how to tackle the challenge whilst recognizing that humour can be found in every situation'
Joe Thompson, former MD, Virgin Holidays

'This book takes away the stigma associated with redundancy and turns it into an opportunity to rethink your career and discover work that works for you'
Alison Grade, author of *The Freelance Bible*

Eleanor Tweddell worked in the corporate world for over twenty years, in senior management positions for companies including Virgin Atlantic, Costa Coffee and Vodafone, until she was made redundant. This inspired her to start her own company, Another Door, to work with individuals and organisations to provide advice and support through redundancy.

Why Losing Your Job Could be the Best Thing That Ever Happened to You

Five Simple Steps to Thrive after Redundancy

Eleanor Tweddell

BUSINESS

PENGUIN BUSINESS

UK | USA | Canada | Ireland | Australia
India | New Zealand | South Africa

Penguin Business is part of the Penguin Random House group of companies
whose addresses can be found at global.penguinrandomhouse.com.

Penguin
Random House
UK

First published 2020
001

Copyright © Eleanor Tweddell, 2020

The moral right of the author has been asserted

Set in 12.5/16pt Dante MT Std
Typeset by Jouve (UK), Milton Keynes
Printed and bound in Great Britain by Clays Ltd, Elcograf S.p.A.

A CIP catalogue record for this book
is available from the British Library

ISBN: 978-0-241-45897-6

Follow us on LinkedIn: https://www.linkedin.com/company/penguin-connect/

www.greenpenguin.co.uk

To Hannah.

Hoping you never need this book,
but if you do, you know it's going to be OK.

Contents

'When one door closes, another door opens, but we so often look so long and so regretfully upon the closed door, that we do not see the ones which open for us.'

Alexander Graham Bell

You should get used to hearing this quote, or a version of it. I have no idea how many times I heard it from well-intentioned friends and awkward colleagues in the first few weeks after I was made redundant. Which doors do they mean? And where do they lead to? It may have become a painful cliché, but Alexander Graham Bell did have a point. You may feel like a door has closed (or in some cases slammed in your face) but, by the end of this book, you'll have gained the ideas, tools and actions to take control of the situation and even recognize it for the opportunity it might be. Another door will open and, when it does, you'll be equipped with the insight and confidence to stride straight through it.

My business, Another Door, was born from my frustrations, my worry and my doubts, followed by my hope, new ideas, the feeling of possibility and, finally, gaining the courage to take action. There is opportunity all around you; you just need to want to see it.

How to Use This Book

This book is designed to guide you through the ups and downs that result after you are made redundant. (I concentrate on redundancy, since that is my experience, but the advice is generally applicable however you have come to lose your job.) Dip in and dip out and you will find the support and expertise to help get you back on your feet again – whatever that might look like. Get scribbling; make notes in the margins, highlight, cross out, make this book your own.* If you need more space then use a notepad.

Some pages will connect with you more than others and some you will want to come back to more than once. Everyone's journey to re-employment is different. You may find that this is a brilliant time to stop and reflect and take a different path in your career. You might want to pursue a new passion. You could start your own business, go part-time or give up work altogether. Losing your job could be an opportunity to consider what is important to you. It could be the best thing that ever happened to you.

The good news is that by choosing to read this book you're already taking action to learn and grow from this experience. That's half the battle. Adopting an open

---

* Unless this is a library copy!

mindset is fundamental to getting back on your feet and thriving after a redundancy.

I begin the book in Part 1, **Shock**, by examining the first few days or weeks after becoming unemployed. It's a confusing, anxious time. The feeling of rejection can be overwhelming. You might feel as if your life has been interrupted or that you were heading in one direction and now the road ahead is uncertain and your future unknown. Overcoming shock is the first step to moving on. This section will help you tune into how you are feeling and show you how to give yourself space to lean into those feelings as part of the process of getting back on your feet. Your milestone will be the moment you let go of what has happened and start to think of your future.

In Part 2, **Stuck**, I focus on the period between the door closing and you opening another one. You've accepted what has happened but you're not sure what to do next. The feeling of being stuck means you're receptive to possibilities, ready to make things happen, aware that change has to come. The milestone moment is when you start to have ideas, get curious and begin thinking about what you might do next.

In Part 3, **Slow, Slow, Go**, I address the most common reaction to losing your job, which is to rush into job-search mode. Fuelled by the adrenalin rush of pure panic, it's tempting to launch straight into LinkedIn and send off a hundred applications at once. The aim of this section is to help you to focus your regained energy into making progress and not simply being busy. 'Slow, Slow, Go' will help you focus your thinking to achieve clarity about what it is you want to do and turn your new-found energy into action. The milestone moment is when you are absolutely certain what you want to do and why.

In Part 4 I focus on how you become **Unstuck**. Here you will find the tools to plan effectively and build the skills and support network that will help you turn your dreams into reality. Now that you have a view of what you want to do, you can create a plan of action and begin to take steps towards your goal. Intentional action focuses your energy on the elements that will produce results. You've done all the thinking, now you will act and put your plan into place. Your milestone moment is when you share your plans with your support network with absolute clarity and conviction.

Finally, Part 5 – the best bit – is where you learn to **Thrive**. The great news is that you've got through the hard part, you've done the work and now it's time to enjoy the results. This section will help you stay focused, over-come setbacks and enact your plan with confidence. You've made it through one of the biggest challenges of your pro-fessional career and even managed to turn it into a positive experience. Your milestone moment is starting to see all your hard work pay off; your planning is beginning to bear fruit and you are landing the goals you set out to achieve.

I'm glad to have you here.

I'll be with you every step of the way.

Part 1

Shock

You've Been Dumped

CASE STUDY: My story

I put the phone down. I was suddenly very aware of the silence. My phone had one text message from my husband and daughter: 'Good Luck Mummy. We love you.' I instantly felt a wave of guilt wash over me. It was 20 December. And because of me they were going to have a bad Christmas. And a bad New Year. In fact, a bad year altogether. The call had been quick: 'You've been unsuccessful. You haven't got the job and so, as a result, you are being made redundant.' The company had given me the opportunity to avoid redundancy by applying for a similar role which I'd failed to secure, and so I was out. The phone call continued, but I don't know what else was said. My mind had gone blank after hearing those words. I was feeling numb. 'You are being made redundant.' That is all that kept going round in my head.

Just three months earlier I had been planning my maternity leave with my boss. I was excited by finding someone to cover my role, preparing for my second child and planning for a house move. Little did I know that just twelve weeks later I would have lost both my baby and my job and be in grave danger of losing my mind as well. I sat on the sofa and cried. Wiping tears away, I logged on to Indeed, LinkedIn, Reed et al. and registered for any jobs, in any area, doing anything, as soon as possible. Within three weeks I'd had thirty-two rejection emails, two interviews for jobs that offered less money and responsibility than the one I had just left and my self-esteem was evaporating faster than smoke up a chimney. I was losing focus, losing courage, losing myself. This had hit me hard – much harder than I'd thought.

My story of redundancy will be different from yours. Everyone's journey through this process is unique. Since this terrifying moment, I've worked with hundreds of clients who have experienced redundancy in all its myriad shapes and forms. But all the stories I have heard have something in common, and that is that losing your job is one of life's great challenges. Just as with bereavement or divorce, there will follow a period during which you will experience utter shock. Redundancy hurts. It has the power to trigger feelings of worthlessness, fear, panic, guilt and shame. You may feel that everything you've been working towards has been for nothing or that your carefully laid plans for the future lie in ruins. This section will help you understand and accept these feelings, which is the fastest way – indeed, the only way – for you to move on to the next stage of your journey.

Why does redundancy happen?

The world of work is changing. Businesses are constantly having to adapt to remain competitive. CEOs and their senior leadership teams have to make big decisions in order to keep their jobs (they've got mortgages too). The organizational structure of businesses is changing to make them more reactive to change. Many larger, bureaucratic companies are moving from hierarchical, top-down triangles to highly flexible, federal organizations in which separate divisions are given autonomy to make their own decisions. Where salaried, full-time staff once comprised the majority of the workforce, our teams now are made up of freelancers, project managers or flexi-workers hired to fulfil specific skill requirements.

Being made redundant can feel like a really bad relationship break-up. Anyone who has been dumped will know the feeling. Your partner seems distant, avoiding eye-contact, being evasive. You start to worry that you've done something wrong. Your gut tells you that there's a problem. Then, all of a sudden you hear, 'It's not you, it's me,' and it's all over.

At first, you might think there's still hope. Perhaps they're just having a bad day. It could be a mistake. They might change their minds. Or you might feel angry. How dare they! What gives them the right? Or you might feel instant worry. What are you going to do? Even if you saw it coming, you may feel numb. Not sure what to think.

Just like a break-up, losing your job can trigger many difficult emotions. But, it really *is* them, not you. Organizations implement redundancies for many different reasons: the company might be struggling, they might need to reshape to keep up with competition, changing technology, repurposing. They have probably explained this to you already, but these might not be the answers you need. Remember, it's your job that has been made redundant, not you. The sooner you accept that, the quicker you can move on, focusing on what you have rather than what you've lost. Holding on to your anger can stop you moving on. As you might block your ex-partner's calls, or unfriend them on social media, choosing to focus your attention on the future rather than dwelling on the past is the first step. You can achieve closure by spending more time thinking about you.

When redundancy is personal

Throughout the book I'll stress that redundancy is not personal, and that is almost always the case. But, it could be, it could just be – ah, this is awkward! – well, it might be that you actually got fired under the guise of being made redundant. And then it *is* personal. We aren't meant to admit that this happens but it does. Sometimes, rather than have a difficult performance management conversation and start the tiresome-for-all-parties review process, it's just easier to make the role redundant. Problem solved.

Of course, the problem hasn't been solved at all, just

kicked down the road. Managers who choose to take this route may console themselves that they are giving their employee an easier, softer way out by concealing the real reason for their dispatch but, in reality, the ex-employee will never know why they lost their job. They can't learn from the experience. The company has robbed them of the chance to self-reflect and improve.

Most redundancies are large scale, and this is a good indication that there is no hidden agenda, but if your role was singled out, you might want to reflect on whether your 'redundancy' might have been performance related. Were you meeting the expectations of the company? Did you ask for help? It might be difficult to accept, but the only way you can own this situation is to learn from it.

In summary, sometimes redundancy is personal, but if you are big enough, and strong enough, you can still turn it into an opportunity. Right, now we've got that out the way – let's move on!

Change is All Around – Lean into It

Change is all around and ever present in our lives. As well as the shape of businesses changing, there is a definitive movement of people wanting more flexibility, more purpose, more meaning from their professions. The traditional career paths are disappearing. We are working for much longer as our life expectancy extends. Where we work and for how long has become less rigid. In short, we are entering a new era of work. There are many reasons why redundancies happen and some of them may have contributed to your own situation. In many ways, the reason you lost your job doesn't matter. What matters is how you respond. Adopting an open mindset and practising self-reflection – 'a curiosity mindset' – will fast-track your recovery and get you back in control of your career.

The Practical Stuff

What a lot of people don't tell you about being made redundant is the flurry of admin it creates. You will need to find out when your last day will be, how your exit will be handled, whether you require legal representation – the list is endless. Putting your practical hat on during this time can be a welcome distraction from the emotional turmoil that is bubbling under the surface. You've likely gone from an overflowing inbox, a full calendar and a busy office to blank lists, silent phones and an empty room with only daytime TV to keep you occupied. This is where your experience kicks in. You managed to organize your workload in the past; you need to apply those skills now. This is the biggest project you've worked on to date. Stop panicking. Start writing your list. Here are some ideas to get you started.

Your in-work benefits

Jot down a list of the job-related benefits that you received. Do you even know all of them? You may need to consult your HR representative. Here are some suggestions:

- Company car
- Train tickets/bus pass
- Pension

- Health insurance
- Shares/bonuses
- Gym membership
- Cycle-to-work scheme
- Childcare vouchers
- Laptop
- Phone
- Email address
- Company discounts/partnership deals

This might feel depressing but starting this process will help you feel better and avoid any shocks once you leave work. You might even find that detaching from these ties feels liberating!

Your monthly outgoings

Losing your job can be a huge financial hit, but you can protect yourself by planning ahead. Establishing what you spend each month, and where you can cut down, will minimize the impact on your bank balance. Write down how much comes in and out of your account each month, listing all your bills and direct debits as well as estimates for living costs like food and entertainment. Where can you make savings? Are there memberships or direct debits that you can cancel or freeze until you are more financially stable? For example:

- **Mortgage** – You should tell your provider about your changed circumstances. They may be able to offer help in the form of a 'payment holiday' or other scheme.
- **Utility bills** – Do you have any tariffs that can be reduced by moving to a better deal?
- **Memberships** – Be honest, are you really making the most of that gym membership?
- **Loans and credit cards** – What are your minimum payments? Can you talk to a specialist to help streamline your debts?

Money worries – quick fixes

Money worries can become overwhelming when you're out of work. Here are a few tips to help you.

- Crunch your numbers, find out what the reality of your situation is rather than just having a feeling about it. Know how much money you have, what you need, and when you need to start earning again.
- If you need to start earning money quickly here are a few things you can do:
  - Post on LinkedIn that you are actively looking for a new job.

- Tell people you are available for contracts and projects in your areas of expertise.
- Register with a few recruitment agencies that closely match your core skillset. You could consider working part-time to keep the money coming in while still leaving yourself space to think about the future.
- Offer to do mentoring and voluntary work. This will help take your mind off your money worries and could lead to unexpected opportunities.

Legal advice

This book provides no advice about the legal side of losing your job, or your rights under employment legislation. Start by consulting your HR department, who should be able to provide you with a breakdown of next steps, timelines and guidance. You may need to find a solicitor to help you negotiate any particularly difficult situations. Find out whether their fees are included in your company's redundancy package. See also the Resources section at the end of the book.

The Change Curve

Now that you've got a bit more organized on the practicalities, it's time to pay attention to yourself. Bottling up your emotions at this time will only make things worse. You have gone straight to the front of the emotional redundancy rollercoaster, hopped on, seat belt fastened, and you are now charging along the Change Curve theme-park ride. Have you paid any attention to how you are feeling yet? You might feel ashamed, lost, tired. You might even be slightly excited. Whatever you are feeling it's all energy consuming, so tune in, and be honest about how you feel.

Owning the change

The change curve, which was devised by Swiss-American psychiatrist Elisabeth Kübler-Ross, is used in organizations to help people manage through change. This curve reflects the five stages of grief: denial, anger, bargaining, depression, acceptance. The five stages are a useful way to think about stages of change and how we can help ourselves move through them. According to Kübler-Ross, the stages are 'transferable to different ways and degrees and may vary from person to person'. Being made redundant is a form of grief. You are letting go of something you valued, an important part of your life, and someone else decided to take it away. You are experiencing loss. It makes sense that the change curve resonates and helps you move through it.

The Kübler-Ross change curve

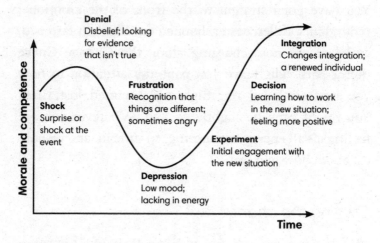

The Kübler-Ross change curve can help you understand your emotions and check in to see where you are along the process. Take a look at the graph and mark where you think best describes your current emotional state.

At first sight, the graph seems to have a start and a finish, but the reality is that the journey isn't so bounded. When life throws you a curve ball, your curve is not a beautiful smooth pear-shaped silhouette; instead, the curve starts to meander, small curves break away from the main one, they loop around, they cause landslides, they then calm and become slow-moving beautiful streams innocently heading off to meet the sea, and then they hit rocks again, splash around, hope for a calm day so things can regroup. Not so much of a curve as a tangled ball of string, unravelling everywhere, getting into a knot and tripping people up, especially you. Rarely will you feel so many emotions in one month, week, day, hour – hope, anger, grief, delight, relief, terror, optimism, fear.

The real curve ball change curve

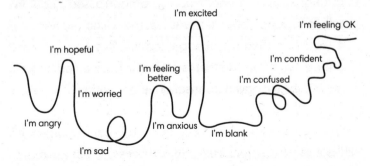

Curve ball curve

- I'm excited
- I'm feeling OK
- I'm hopeful
- I'm confident
- I'm feeling better
- I'm confused
- I'm worried
- I'm angry
- I'm anxious
- I'm blank
- I'm sad

Being made redundant can feel like one tangled mess. One minute a hopeful calm composure, the next minute blind panic. Embrace the curve. What you are feeling right now is right. The curve keeps moving and so will you. You won't stay in this place for ever.

Guilt and Shame

When I received my phone call to tell me I no longer had a job and I was being made redundant, the first thing I felt was guilt. Guilty I'd let my family down, my husband, my daughter. Guilty I'd not done more to try to keep the job. Guilty, that, because of me, there would be strain and pressure on the family. And with five days to go until Christmas, our festivities would now have a different vibe. But why the guilty feeling?

> **CASE STUDY – Anne**
> 'I felt ashamed of being made redundant. I kept running through it in my head, I was so embarrassed I couldn't talk to anyone about it. It was just me telling me how bad it was. And then I spoke to a counsellor. And my world changed. I still felt elements of shame but worked through my reality. I'm now a counsellor helping others.'

Guilt and shame live very close together, along with self-doubt, fear, anger and unworthiness. What a street to live on! Lucy Power, a therapeutic coach, explains that guilt is an emotional warning sign. Its purpose is to let us know when we've done something wrong, to help us develop a better sense of our behaviour and how it affects ourselves and others. It prompts us to think about what we did so that we don't make the same mistake again. But what if our behaviour isn't something that needs examining or changing? Then it becomes unhealthy, because our guilt is serving no rational purpose. You can't learn from the experience if it wasn't your fault. And that guilt releases itself and morphs into fear, disappointment and shame. The reality is that losing your job is rarely your fault. You can't shoulder the blame.

Guilt and shame can provide you with valuable thinking time. Psychologists even talk about guilt and shame providing useful energy to alert the brain that you need to find solutions and create ideas.

In their book *The Upside of Your Dark Side*, Todd Kashdan and Robert Biswas-Diener talk about how

being overly positive can make you gullible. In one study, people who were in a bad mood did much better at detecting deception than happy people. This goes back to the cave people. If you were suspicious, anxious, overanalysed, always ready for the worst-case scenario . . . then you were more likely to keep out of harm's way or find a way to avoid or get out of tricky situations.

So, your dark feeling is giving you the strength to get going again and fight back. That might be the reason why so many people find the strength to create something completely different for themselves when they get made redundant. Your perceived guilt can propel not the practical side of getting another job but the intentional side of finding a solution, and will help you to be braver than you would have been had you stayed in your comfortable role. People also talk about the feeling that they have 'nothing to lose' and so try things with the gusto of 'What's the worst that can happen?'

Guilt can be the catalyst of change

The guilt of losing your job might result in you trying to redress the balance in your life. As an example, if your guilt involves your family then you might start to create more quality time with them.

CASE STUDY – Susan

'When my husband got made redundant he went through some very low days, then one day he just started being really helpful around the house. I got back home from work and he'd sorted out the cupboards, cooked a nice meal, bought me some flowers . . . I wondered what was going on! I don't get flowers every day but I feel like I have a more caring husband now.'

'Guilt is a bad feeling about stuff you have done and haven't done. Shame is a bad feeling about who you are and who you are not,' says Lucy Power. 'Guilt creeps in as you start to wonder if you did do something, or if it was your fault.'

How you were treated when you were made redundant might have a huge effect on how you handle it. There is a difference between being told by text that you've lost your job and being invited to sit with your manager and talk about it. But how it was handled is not your issue. How you move on is.

Revenge

Guilt, shame, frustration can all turn into anger. You might still be thinking bad thoughts of the people involved. You might be wishing a lot of bad luck on your ex-employer. You might be plotting revenge.

You might not care that much. If this is you, I give you lots of hand clapping and admiration, because as Francis Bacon once said, 'In taking revenge, a man is but even with his enemy; but in passing it over, he is superior.' During this period of anger, we can't get enough of the joy of finding out how badly things are going wrong back in the office, that targets are being missed and budgets exceeded, that new bosses are turning out to be very incompetent. 'It's my one pleasure right now,' you say. 'Don't take it away from me with your positive thinking, and your "just move on" advice.'

You are a human being and sometimes bad thoughts creep in, but red raw anger that is focused around your ex-employer is wasted energy. Use that emotion to power your next move. You don't have to show anyone how hurt you are. You can demonstrate your commitment to moving on by putting your energy into your next move. As another great philosopher, Frank Sinatra, once said, 'the best revenge is a massive success'.

The author Jim Grant, who you might know better by his pen name Lee Child, was involved with more than

40,000 hours of TV production with Granada over eighteen years. He knew how to tell a story. He wrote thousands of links, trailers, commercials and news stories. He was made redundant in 1995 at the age of forty as a result of organization restructuring. He decided to see an opportunity where others might have seen a crisis and, the story goes, he bought £5 worth of paper and pencils and sat down to write a book, *Killing Floor*, the first in the Jack Reacher series. As he explains in *Lee Child Quotes and Believes*, 'My question was how to stay inside the world of entertainment without actually getting another job. I felt the only logical answer was to become a novelist. I wrote the first book – driven by some very real feelings of desperation – and it worked.'

Use your revenge as fuel, not to prove anything to anyone, and not to waste your emotion on others, but to show yourself exactly what you are made of.

Hibernation

A common reaction to redundancy is to feel depressed and low on drive. We might not want to face the world and choose instead to hide ourselves away and avoid awkward conversations with friends and family. Even picking up the phone might feel like too much to handle at this stage. Your inner voice can tell you stories about how you're not good enough. Redundancy hibernation is the point where we just can't generate enough energy to go outside so we lock ourselves away.

When animals hibernate, they are preserving their energy ready for spring, when they burst out and roll about in plants and mud and go hunting and rebuild their dens and go in search of new buddies. Maybe we can learn something from the animals. If you want to hibernate for a while, then do it. If you need some space, away from the world, that's OK. Rest. Preserve energy. And when your spring comes, you'll be ready to burst outside, roll about in plants and mud, and create your new life.

A Change of Role at Home

Your career role might not be the only role that starts to change.

> **CASE STUDY – Andy**
> 'I went from the "breadwinner", working away four days a week, back at weekends to play with the kids, to stay-at-home dad, making sandwiches for the kids' lunches, doing after-school activity runs, making dinner, doing the shopping. It was a big wake-up call on the first day I had to go to the supermarket – and I didn't know where the nearest one was!'

If you go on gardening leave, and start to spend each day at home, you might find things begin to change with your relationships, whether it's with family or friends. Just like the whole redundancy experience, try to keep on top of things. True friends will remain true friends. There may be a change in how you interact – how you meet, the things you do – but you are still fundamentally the same person. It's a similar experience for anyone going through a life change, when people get married, have children, move house, swap jobs – life does its shuffle and some people stick with you, others fall out of the pack. Andy's experience reflects this:

'I was part of a group of friends that earned very well, played very well. When I got made redundant I found it hard to justify spending money on weekends away, big drinking nights out. I declined a few events and within a few weeks I noticed I'd stopped being invited. Half of me was relieved, as I was feeling pressure, but I also felt sad. They were a close group of friends. I still see a few, but we've all moved on and my life priorities are very different now.'

Gardening leave, and time between jobs, is your time. You are choosing how to fill it. No one has taken away your ability to make decisions and choose what you do every morning. The 'inbetweener' time is only a temporary state. Choosing to embrace your time, to take it on, and use it as you wish will give you a world of opportunities and you might see things you've never noticed before. As Andy found, there can be some upside:

'This year I'm really looking forward to Christmas. I got made redundant in September. I set myself a goal to return to work in February. I've been using my spare time well. This year I've bought all the kids' Christmas presents. For the first year (ever) I will know what they've got from Santa, what the presents are under the tree. I never had given a thought to how I felt about me just looking on at the hustle taking place on Christmas Day. Christmas Day had been just another day off. I'd work right up to Christmas Eve, get home by

5 p.m. and my wife had everything ready – the decorations, the shopping, presents were wrapped, friends invited round for drinks, family invited round on Boxing Day. My role, really, was an extension of my work. I just got given my schedule by my wife (personal life), my PA (work life), and my role was to turn up, say the right things at the right time. Thinking about it was very transitional and passive. I was there, but I wasn't part of it. It's not a great feeling, thinking about it now. My kids are nine and eleven. This year is going to be so different. I'm not just in the room, I'll be IN the room.'

Create Your Line to Take

Telling people that you've been made redundant can be difficult. It can feel embarrassing, like admitting failure. Most people don't know the right way to respond, which can lead to some awkwardness. If you haven't worked on the story you are telling yourself, the act of telling the story to others will begin to hurt, and by 'story' I mean the narrative you're happy to share with people. Whether that is, 'Yes, I'm devastated. I don't know what to do, I'm still processing it,' or, 'I can't wait to use my redundancy package to go on a very long holiday,' or anything in between, now is a good time to activate your PR plan, your pre-prepared response or, as I like to call it, your Line to Take (LTT). Not only does it matter what story you are proactively telling, it also matters how you are reacting. As you start to tell people you've been made redundant you are going to be asked questions. If you think about how you are going to answer them, your answers will help you move on quicker as well as help confirm the story you are telling yourself. You won't waste energy worrying about what to say or dealing with emotions afterwards.

What is your LTT?

Let's practise.

Question:

- 'Oh hi, how are you? How is the job search going?'

Possible LTTs:

- 'A few things in the pipeline, I don't want to rush into things' (keep yourself in control).
- 'Down to the last two, so feeling good about whatever the result' (affirmations).
- 'It's actually going really rubbish' (it might be true but won't help you or the person who has asked).
- 'It's OK. Keeping all doors open. How was your holiday to Malta?' (use deflection and move the conversation back to them).

Having a strong LTT can also help you move on and work as a marketing tool. As you form a view of what you want to happen next, build it into your LTT. We'll go into this more further on in the book, so for now just view the question 'How are you?' as a vote of support.

And just like the best politicians, take control of any

answers, return to your agenda – and be quick to move on.

Write down your LTT and practise using it. You will be prepared for any questioning, however innocent or not so much, and remain in control.

The Gift of Cliché

There are a moments in your life that seem ridden with clichés. Getting married, being single, having a baby, getting divorced, being burgled, moving house and being made redundant. Clichés occur when something is so familiar to us that we don't think creatively about our response and instead rely on cut-and-paste answers.

- 'I've got a cold.' – 'Yeah, there's a lot of it going around.'
- 'My house was burgled.'– 'Oh no! My neighbour's cousin was burgled a few years ago too; terrible, hope they didn't take much.'

Most cliché-givers mean well. Their advice is drawn from set pieces, well-trodden paths, and, as Russell Brand says, 'things that people say when they can't think quick enough to say anything else'. Clichés are painful to hear because they rarely offer much in the way of comfort, wisdom or advice. And often they are totally untrue, or at least the sentiment is either false or inane – 'Everything happens for a reason,' for example.

When you start to tell people you've been made redundant, you're taking a big step to say those words out loud. For some, it feels like you are telling the world, 'Oh hello, I'm a bit shit, I've been caught out, so they've sacked me,

'Cliché saves us from thinking.'

Russell Brand

nice to meet you.' And seven times out of ten the response will be a cliché.

After a while clichés start to sap your energy. You are constantly engaging in lazy conversations that have no depth or value and certainly offer you no help or support.

Of course, most people are just trying to do their best, and they really do want to say something that can help and support you. As frustrating and disheartening as it can be, it's not about the response of the person. It's about where you are right at that moment. And the things you want to receive and the things you want to block.

If you are in shock, whatever form that takes, then you are probably not ready to think about a positive outcome. You are still wallowing, and not only that, you are getting used to wallowing. You do not want to hear there may be a good solution, and you do not want to hear someone trivializing your situation with what sounds like a throwaway comment.

We've all dished up the odd cliché at one time or another. Clichés are mostly delivered with the intent to support and show compassion. People want to help, they want to empathize, but when stuck for things to say clichés are an automated, safe option. Most of the time they at least incorporate a bit of hope, so open yourself up to accepting that glimmer of encouragement as a sign that the cliché is intended to support, and is a signal that the person is on your side. Take the cliché in and use it. Use it to help you smile, use it to help you refocus, use it to help you get on with life. Clichés are important to deal with because if you react negatively to something that is offered as support, it will keep you feeling stuck. It might even make you feel worse. An early rethink of clichés can save a lot of wasted time and energy spent getting frustrated by the wrong things.

I remember the day someone said to me, 'Ah well, when one door closes, another door opens . . .' I remember my thoughts on hearing this cliché gift.

I cannot type them here.

I remember as that person walked away, off to sit in their cosy seat, in their cosy office, to carry on with their cosy job that they'd managed to keep – I remember thinking bad thoughts all afternoon. That exchange did not contribute much to me moving into a more positive position.

But was it the cliché gifter's fault? No. It was mine.

And once I got over myself, and blew away the cliché, I kept a small part of it. In amongst the frustration, my usual curious mind wondered, 'Actually, what is that saying all about?' I googled it. I disappeared down a rabbit hole reading about Alexander Graham Bell.

And a small idea appeared . . .

From frustration, annoyance, hope, googling, reading, to an idea, and now a business.

So, the next time a cliché comes to greet you, choose. Choose to blow it away, spend no more time on it, let it go and get on with your vibe, or choose to let it in, embrace it, take its intention onboard.

Cliché bingo

Here is a game we can all play. Whenever you are on the receiving end of a cliché you score points as indicated below. See how many points you've scored after a month of telling people. My score was 270.

- Everything happens for a reason (2 points). *Most hated cliché. (Try telling that to someone who's just been given six months to live.) However, good things can happen from life's curve balls; you have to make something happen by finding an opportunity.*
- You were better than that job (10 points).
- Every cloud has a silver lining (20 points).
- Plenty more fish in the sea (20 points).
- All's well that ends well (30 points).
- Chin up (30 points).
- There will be something better around the corner (40 points).
- Worse things happen at sea (40 points).
- Que Sera Sera (50 points).
- You have a roof over your head, could be worse (50 points).
- One door closes, another door opens (100 points).

Exit with Grace

A company I once worked for called the last part of its employee experience 'exit with grace'. They were keen on making people redundant every quarter so it was very apt that this was part of the experience of working there. As much as 'exit with grace' can be interpreted as 'shift on quietly please', it has benefits for you too.

It's not about not causing trouble or sticking up for yourself but rather being aware that how you leave might impact you later. You don't know when or where you might meet ex-colleagues again. If you are going to raise issues, ask for further conversations, do it, but do it with grace. Leaving with bad feeling will stay with you a lot longer than any of the people who remain at the organization.

CASE STUDY – Roger

'I couldn't believe the man who had caused me so much stress for years in my previous job, who had eventually made me redundant, was now in my new place of work, talking to my boss. The rumour was he was about to become our new director. My heart sank. I loved this new job, away from him. How were they even thinking about employing him? On his first day, he came over to my desk. "I recognize that face," he said. "Great to have you on the team." It sounded genuine and I was so confused. I hated him. Until I thought about it. I never caused a fight with him, I did discuss that I felt under pressure, but I never made it personal. He just didn't associate bad feelings with me. And thank God it worked out.'

It's a really thin line between sticking up for yourself versus causing trouble versus keeping quiet. There is no right advice here. You must do what you think is right at the time. The key is not to make decisions, and especially not to act on them, from an emotional state. If you feel you are reacting, walk away, pause, delay the meeting. Compose and be proactive. I know there are many examples of unfair dismissals, and dubious reasons for your redundancy but you must be clear what you want to get out of appealing. Be clear on why you want to use energy fighting rather than using energy to move on.

Gardening Leave

> It is my very sad duty to tell you that Derek has decided to leave us to pursue new ventures. Derek has been a huge contributor to the success of the team and we will miss his wit and wisdom. Derek will be on gardening leave with immediate effect, spending valuable time with his family. We wish him every luck in the future.

Your employer, now ex-employer, may ask you not to come into work, or to work at home, to go on 'gardening leave'. Although you are not physically constrained, and you are released back into the world on full pay (up to an agreed final date), you aren't completely free. You can be called back to work at any time. You definitely can't start another job, and you really shouldn't be talking to competitors. All you can really be doing is . . . gardening.

When I was on gardening leave, my curious mind got me wondering about the origin of the term. (Yes I know, you do find yourself with the most abstract of distractions when you have time on your hands!)

I discovered that it might well have originated in the British Civil Service, where 'gardening leave' became a euphemism for suspension as an employee who was pending an investigation into their conduct would often request to be out of the office on special leave instead.

Another possible origin was during the First World

War, when soldiers suffering from 'shell shock' (what we now know as PTSD) would be sent home on medical leave. As part of their rehabilitation they were encouraged to engage in simple but productive tasks such as growing vegetables. They would still be on the military payroll but played no active part in the war.

The term is now firmly associated in many countries with being made redundant, and with the need to get you out of the office as quickly as possible to avoid awkwardness and allow those staying to move on quickly without guilt.

So, you are getting paid for doing nothing? In theory, that might sound great to you, the ultimate dream even, but the reality is that it's very difficult to enjoy getting paid to do nothing. Even for those who have been dreaming of escape to another world, it's still a shock. You are pulled from your everyday reality of presentations, full inboxes and back-to-back meetings into . . . nothing. No calls, no urgent requests, no one needing you for even the smallest thing. It can all start to feel a bit numbing, a bit lonely and a bit confusing. Suddenly you are powering through the change curve at a rapid rate, still trying to process everything that has happened. It's no wonder you can't enjoy it.

We are programmed to understand the equation work = pay. So, if we are being paid not to work, or to do work that doesn't exist, then we lose our sense of purpose. In David Graeber's *Bullshit Jobs* he explains . . .

'If someone could have told me I'd be OK in the next three months, that I'd find a great job, and have no financial or career worries, then, yes, I would've enjoyed my three months of gardening leave.'

Ann, who now runs her own graphic design studio

working serves a purpose or is meant to do so. Being forced to pretend to work just for the sake of working is an indignity, since the demand is perceived – rightly – as the pure exercise of power for its own sake. So being forced out of work, and losing purpose actually feels like a loss of freedom, not a gain of it.

Because we have attached ourselves, our worth, to titles and statuses, when they are taken away it leaves us exposed, and without a label explaining our capability or purpose we have to find other ways to demonstrate who we are. If we are not disguised as busy employees, then who are we? Up until now our busyness has helped us avoid a lot of awkward issues. And now, with the invisibility cloak of busyness lifted, we might have to start addressing some of them.

Gardening leave, while accepted as better than the alternative of straightforward dismissal, can leave us feeling empty. Is there a way to make the most of it?

A four-week holiday might be a bit extreme for some people. The point is to be brave in the space created. It's not about doing, and being super busy, but it is about being intentional about how you are choosing to use your time (which includes the very OK option of choosing to do nothing). In twelve months' time you could be looking back and wishing you'd made the most of this time off. Try making a list of the best things you could use this

'I went on a four-week backpacking holiday, I would've never thought about it before, but once I knew I had three months' paid leave, I was off. Best thing I ever did.'

Dawn, Another Door member

period for. Have you always wanted to actually do some gardening? Is this a good time to think about your goals? Or do you want to spend it catching up with family, getting fit or doing those DIY jobs you've been putting off? Sort out your Spotify account, clear out that cluttered cupboard, do a charity drop-off.

- Indulge yourself. This is a stressful time so make sure you spend some of your gardening leave recharging and doing things you love.
- Be intentional. Every day get up and decide what you are going to do that day. Not big overwhelming decisions but clear small intentions: 'Today I will just think.' 'Today I will contact five people in my network.' 'Today I will apply for two jobs.' 'Today I will read.' Write down your intention in your notebook, and stick to it. You'll feel the pressure lift, and also that you are making gentle progress.
- It's all going to work out. My apologies for increasing your cliché bingo score, but having faith that something will come along really will help you to relax and get the most out of your gardening leave.

The O Word

Your organization may have offered outplacement support. This is provided by external businesses that deliver workshops, coaching and advice as you leave your job. Some of the services are brilliant, and people have a great experience and benefit hugely. Others can make you feel like you are being processed and add to the undermining feeling that you are just a number. My business, Another Door, was created to support people through redundancy on their own terms, to make them feel human and encouraged to own what happens next. The whole concept of 'outplacement' didn't resonate for me, so this book was created out of a feeling that I didn't have the support I wanted. It's always worth asking your soon-to-be ex-employer what's on offer. You might be offered free quality workshops and coaching that help you move on.

CASE STUDY – Kate

'The first time I got made redundant I felt as though I was being processed, it was an extension of the humiliation of the redundancy. I was allocated ten hours with an adviser. He made me feel worse than sitting in a room alone with my own thoughts. The second time I was made redundant it was a different outplacement company, my adviser was brilliant, full of support and if felt like she genuinely cared.'

If your company offers you outplacement support, accept it. If you want to make redundancy feel like the best thing that ever happened to you, start owning the process as quickly as possible. Of course, you are reading this book, so you've already made a good move towards considering all your options. You are going to be in a great position to make the most of any support offered too, because you'll know what you want, and why. And the chances are you have looked at Another Door. The community learning modules and support provided there work with you to make sure you make the most of any outplacement you are offered. You can use the principles of stick, twist and bust outlined in Part 2 to make the best use of your time and energy. If you want to stick with what you know then focus on CV, interview and job-search services. If you want to try something completely new and start a business then ask for specific support to do that.

Coming Out of Shock

Losing your job has been a shock and it's fine to feel emotional about it. I hope this section will help you to take back control quickly and turn your anxious energy into proactivity and planning. Check in with your emotions and be honest about how you feel. This will enable you to move on and come out of shock as quickly as possible.

Shock top tip – set a small intention each day

Every morning when you wake up, use your notebook to set an intention for the day. These should be small goals to start with. Today I intend to listen to a podcast on my specialism. Today I intend to spend an hour on my website. Today I intend to walk to the park. Write something down every day and it will become a routine. It will focus your energy first thing in the morning and help you concentrate on being proactive and not worrying.

Shock is an immediate response, and embracing the change and allowing yourself to feel emotional is part of the moving-on process. You've accepted it now. So what next?

Part 2

Stuck

Welcome to stuck. This is the next stage of your redundancy journey. You've come a long way. You've accepted that things are going to be changing. It's a shock, yes, but it's OK. It's happened. You've let the suddenness and sadness sink in and begun to get your head around some of the ways in which your life has become different. Now you can start to move forward. The problem is, where to?

During stuck, the moment in your life when you most need energy and drive, you are often left feeling like the tank is empty. It can seem hopeless. But just like any good comeback story this is just the first very necessary step in moving on with purpose. The cyclist who falls off during the race uses a lot more energy trying to get back on the bike and started again than they ever did while in full flow – but that's not to say they don't get back in the saddle and go on to win the race. You might be stuck as to what to do next. But there is good news.

Once you move away from the feeling of shock, anger and frustration and you start to think about the future, even though you might be feeling stuck, then that's progress – you are moving on. Feeling stuck is the start of that process. It is also an acknowledgement that you need some thinking time to regroup, adjust and formulate ideas as to what you are going to do next.

Your stuckness might be simply a lack of knowledge about how to do something.

Your stuckness might be emotional, lacking a sense of direction, feeling lost.

Your stuckness might be a physical thing that's holding you back.

Your stuckness is part of you moving on.

If you feel stuck right now and unsure what to do next, that's a good sign. It means you are taking ownership of your future, you are starting to ask questions, beginning to wonder about the possibilities, question whether this is a sign that maybe you need to be doing something else. At any moment in your life you can feel stuck – it's a normal experience to have – but the fact you are reading this book means you've already taken a step to help you move on, so let's see where this takes you!

Stick, Twist, Bust

As you come out of shock and start to think about what you are going to do next, you might come up with ideas and then more ideas and then more. You might become overwhelmed, even paralysed, by all the choice, and the many possibilities you have come up with. Not to mention *how* you are going to do it. But at least you now have some choices. The luxury of decisions. By the end of this book you'll be clear on how you will move on. To keep it simple, you have three choices:

- **Stick** to your current career path. Take time to think what could be improved. What wasn't working before? Is there something that could make you happier? You could think about location, position, specialism, salary, team, commute time, a different size or kind of organization.
- **Twist** your skills and expertise into a different way of working. You could think about going freelance, becoming a contractor or project worker, taking interim work, training others to do what you do, working for an agency.
- **Bust.** Throw it all in and start again. Go for something completely new. Out of the comfort zone, into your stretch zone. You could think

about retraining, going back to university,
starting your own business. The possibilities
are endless.

During this phase of 'stuckness' you should free up your thinking, don't restrict your ideas, stay curious. Keep doors open, keep on the road of discovery. As you work through this space between one door closing and the next door opening, you'll have moments of high energy, moments of low mood, but you'll keep moving, and at the right moment you'll know whether you want to stick, twist or bust.

Moments of Oh

During stuck, you'll have many moments of *Oh*. These are tiny discoveries or clues to what's going to happen next. They will all contribute to you moving forward so make sure you make a note of them. They might be things like *Oh, I really like being at home to take my daughter to school; perhaps I should search for a career that allows me to fit that in*, or *Oh, I miss being creative, I didn't realize I'd stopped using my creativity in my last role*, or *Oh, I never want to work for a boss that I don't get on with again*. They might be small things or big things but all will be useful in helping you take that next step. The space between a door closing and another opening is about being curious and tuning into moments of *Oh*. You'll read new things, meet new people, learn fresh skills – some will resonate, some won't. Make a note of all your *Oh* moments. Observe them. They are a lesson in themselves. Not everything will be a positive experience but it will be an opportunity to grow.

The Art of Wallowing

Despite wanting to move on, stuck may make you feel like you can't or don't know how to. Now is the time to perfect the art of wallowing. Much like hibernation in the previous section, wallowing is an important part of this process. When was the last occasion you had some time to yourself? Being stuck is OK, for a while. We all need a little bit of self-indulgence. It can be good for us. But like all things good for us we must still treat it with care. There is an art to being a good wallower. Here's how.

In his book *S.U.M.O. (Shut Up, Move On)*, Paul McGee describes this time to wallow as 'hippo time'. Paul says, 'hippo time provides you with the opportunity to experience your emotional lows and to be honest about those feelings. If you deny the negative, you block the road to full positive recovery.' So, this is your opportunity to jump into that mud and have a right good roll around and tune into where you feel you are.

Paul has three tips for quality wallowing:

1. **Be careful who you talk to.** Keep clear of energy zappers, problem hijackers, 'if you want my advicers' and 'it could be worsers', what we need here are 'I'm listeningers, I empathizers, I'm with youers'. It's your wallow time, you can choose who you share your wallowing with. Ideally they

shouldn't jump into the mud with you, you just want someone to be standing on the side with a large towel when you are ready to get out.

2. **Be careful how many people you talk to.**
Remember your LTT. You don't need to share your wallowing with everybody. Yes, you do need wallow buddies but you don't need to share with everyone and anyone. Wallowing is a temporary position; you aren't going to be in the mud for long. It's not about being dishonest, it's about choosing who to wallow with to get the best out of it for you.

3. **Be careful how long your hippo time lasts.**
Don't get used to wallowing. You have to feel like this is a temporary luxury, a bit like going for a spa treatment or to the pub. You can go there, you can even enjoy it while you are there, but you know it's a temporary thing and home time will be soon.

Getting stuck in the mud

Wallow time is there to help you rest, recharge, make you feel better, reset and ready to move on. If you feel like wallow time has left you stuck even deeper in the mud, and in fact dark clouds have now arrived, after a few weeks you should consider going to your doctor or find a counsellor to help you. Don't leave low feelings un-addressed; if you are feeling down, face your feelings head-on. They are perfectly normal. If you're finding your feelings overwhelming, there are plenty of people and organizations that can help. Sometimes a helping hand is all it takes. Being stuck is a temporary issue. Trust yourself that you'll get yourself out of it.

There are many ways to wallow. Some are healthy; others you should be careful not to overindulge in.

Watch-out wallowing
- Shop for stuff you don't need.
- Eat chocolate.
- Drink wine.
- Eat Hobnobs.
- Watch (sad) films.
- Indulge in a Netflix box set.

Healthy wallowing
- Walk, find a view, any view, and stare at the skyline.
- Run.
- Do yoga.
- Listen to a podcast.
- Watch your favourite comedies.
- Read the newspaper from front to back.
- Tidy up 'that' cupboard (and sell the stuff on eBay).

- Have a bath during the day with great music, candles and face pack – yes you too, men!
- Have a good cry.

The art of wallowing involves you being kind to yourself. Easing up a bit. Letting go of a few things that are making you feel bad, that are playing on your mind, that are making you feel low. It's OK to not be OK. For a while, at least. It's time for you to recharge your battery.

Why have hope?

Time to light that beautiful, beaming candle of hope. It's probably been there glimmering away inside you all this time, helping you get through that difficult conversation (*hope this goes well*), that sales pitch (*hope they like it*), that will to get home on time (*hope this traffic moves soon*). Hope is undervalued in our lives where we just want people to be assertive and forward and on it. But it is hope that keeps us all alive, and it's hope that will jumpstart your engine. The first stage of becoming unstuck is to have hope. Hope that things could not just be OK again but be even better than they were before. It might be hard to have hope when you are searching every day for a job and nothing is coming up, when you see the media reporting large-scale job losses and when you are seeing your friends and family struggling to find work.

But when you start to find hope and look for possibilities you discover that they were all around you all along. Look in different places and you will find people doing stuff. Doing stuff that you can do too. They are making a success of it. And not only that, they might be offering to help you do the same. Walk down your high street; you'll see somebody's hope, idea and action right there. Every time you buy something, anything, it started with hope, an idea and action.

- Your hairdresser? They were once an office worker.
- Your teacher? They were once a banker.
- Your fitness instructor? They were once in the army.
- Your business coach? They were once a teacher.
- The person who serves you coffee every morning? They were once a policeman.
- Your manager (who fired you)? They were once nervous at an interview and hoped to get the job.

They all knew they wanted something different. They hoped it might happen, one day. They thought about it, started having ideas. Then one day, they did it. They went for it. So now do you see the possibilities? If they can do it, why not you? The hope that this is going to turn out well can begin to manifest in your thoughts. You can see inspiration all around you, and you now can let it in. Let hope ferment and grow. Instead of thinking 'lucky them', start thinking 'lucky me'. If them, why not me? Rethinking what you do, who you are and why you do things can start to present you with a world of opportunities. And right now it's never been easier to learn, grow, start a business, retrain or start something new. All you need is the time to think about it, the right support and the right mindset. And hope.

Where to Search for a New Beginning

After a good time wallowing, it's time to reset. Your battery has now been charged. It's time to release your energy and see where hope is going to take you. Did you have any ideas while you were wallowing? Are you full of hope, but not sure where to start? Well, start at the easy place. You've already got some clues. The job you have enjoyed (or endured) for the last few years may be disappearing, it may feel out of your hands, but what happens next has you firmly in the driving seat. You have more options than you might know right now.

- **Search for clues in your hobbies.** Do you have a hobby, an interest, a passion? Do you have hidden talents, or talents you already share for free, for fun, for entertainment? What are you really good at? Do you do something that others also need to do, but find hard? What can you help others do?
- **Be inspired by T-shaped thinking.** A concept created in Silicon Valley that helps people use their hobbies and skills to broaden their personal growth. Could your passion for flower arranging influence your next career choice? Could it inspire some further training?

- **Use what you have learned from the job you've just left.** What did you bring to your last role? Were you a problem solver? Did you help people? Did you drive sales? How can you bring this experience to your next role? This isn't about the job description, it's about what you did, how you did it, where you got your energy.

Start collecting your ideas in small steps; make notes, start a blog, start writing on Medium, post your ideas on LinkedIn. Ask your friends and former colleagues to help you, collect feedback. Volunteer your time. Test your learnings. Attend conferences. All these experiences may open doors and help you see the possibilities.

Finding Your Purpose in Your Passion

In your social life you play a role. You are choosing to play that role. You may play that role reluctantly or you may be completely happy to do so. You might be a different you socially than you are at work. Explore who you are away from work and what you do. What skills do you use in your social circles? Organizer, entertainer, supporter? What do you like doing? Tidying up, talking to people, helping people, getting creative, fixing things? Spending time thinking about what you enjoy socially can present you with all kinds of clues and inspiration to discover the things that you thrive on, your hidden talents that people value about you, things that people might want more of . . . And then what? You start to have hope. You start to have ideas. You start to take action.

- **Do you like tidying up?** Marie Kondo 'sparked joy' and built her career around decluttering and sharing her methods online.
- **Do you like fitness?** Joe Wicks, the Body Coach, started with small gatherings at his local park. He is now the go-to person for the '15-minute HIIT' body transformation programme and a bestselling author.
- **Are you an artist?** Kia Cannon, Sticks and Ink on Instagram, started sharing her career change

to be an artist, sharing her story, sharing her paintings, sharing behind the scenes. She is now a creative coach and artist.

Marie, Joe and Kia all had a passion that gave them an idea and they acted on it. They all started off being curious about their social strengths, their enjoyment zone, and they followed their energy to develop these as (mega-successful) careers. You have so much more to offer the world. So much more skill and knowledge that can help others. Open up, get curious, search everywhere for ideas and inspiration. Maybe it's not just about finding a new job but about finding your purpose.

What is Your Talent?

Do you know what your talent is? Do you know what you are really good at? Do you know what other people think your talent is? We can easily list what we are bad at – go on, think of five things you're really useless at. Now think of five things you are really good at. It's harder to think of things we are good at because we are naturally self-critical. Try this exercise to help get some ideas. Start with what you enjoy. Note your ideas down on a pad.

- What did you enjoy about your job?
- What do you love doing in your downtime?
- What do you enjoy talking about?
- What are you passionate about?
- What do people say you do well?

If you find it hard to answer these questions, have a think about when you read a newspaper or book, watch TV or scroll social media; what do you enjoy watching, reading, listening to? Is there a theme?

Your talent might be close to your passion. And just because you aren't skilled or trained doesn't mean you can't learn. So, looking at what you enjoy can provide an important clue to what your next steps should look like for your career.

Your talents, whether known to you right now or hidden (and known to others), will be your foundations to help you not just move on, but to make your next move the best thing you ever did.

Flip Your Mind

If this is about managing how you grow and work on your personal development, then it starts with your mind. So many things happen to us that are out of our hands but we always have control of how we respond. At the DO Lectures I attended while on gardening leave, David Hieatt talked about 'the power of reframing' to help us use that control to positive, powerful effect. How many times have we written ourselves off with a negative thought?

I've missed the bus this morning, today is going to be a bad day. Done. Let bad day commence. If you allow yourself to start thinking it, you will believe it and it will become true. If you miss the bus and think you'll use this time at the stop to call home, or that maybe it wasn't even the right bus, or better still not give it any thought and just get the next bus, then your day will continue in positive openness.

In *Designing Your Life*, Bill Burnett and Dave Evans use reframing to look at failure differently, to look at fear differently, to look at guilt differently. They challenge a change of thought from the negative connotations to the positive possibilities.

- **From** I am not smart enough **to** I don't know much but I can learn.

- **From** I am too much of an introvert to be
  successful **to** I have unique skills that are
  valuable to people.

When you start reframing, your story starts to change. Instead of being immersed in all the reasons why things can't, won't, don't happen, you start to see all the things that might, that can, that will. In doing this process we rewrite our story; we rewrite our thoughts.

We are programmed to stay in our comfort zone. To flip your mind, you have to work on it. It takes you constantly reminding yourself. *There may be another way of looking at this. There may be another way to feel about this. Reframe. Maybe there is a different version of the story I'm telling myself. Maybe that story can make me feel better than I do now.*

You can train yourself to reframe. Before you react, ask yourself, is there a different way? The more you do this, the more used to it you'll get. Then one day you'll just do it naturally. You'll notice a negative thought creeping into your brain and you'll flip it. If you notice your internal voice shouting loudly about how bad things are, how you aren't good enough, how you can't do something – think *flip it* and see what happens next.

Your job became redundant, you own what happens next. By flipping your thoughts and the way you think about situations and circumstances, you are taking back

'We can't change events; we have to change how we interpret and react to them.'
David Hieatt, DO Lectures

control. In an interview, Gareth Southgate, the England men's football team manager, was asked how the team prepared for penalty shootouts. His reply: 'We worked on owning the process.'

Southgate talks about several things that meant he could shape the way the team thought about situations so that they felt in control.

- **Keeping calm.** Taking your time, giving yourself space, slowing down under pressure.
- **Preparing to be successful.** Assuming a positive outcome means you're more likely to make it happen. Southgate says, 'When something goes wrong, you have to know it doesn't finish you.' Indeed, Southgate himself missed an important penalty in Euro '96 but went on to become the England manager.
- **Dressing the part.** Southgate says, 'Owning it is all about attitude, so dress to win, dress to get you in the zone.' You can help your frame of mind by putting on your 'power' suit. Don't spend your day in pyjamas; get dressed every morning and keep yourself in the game.

Flipping your mind, changing the way you see things, will mean you are in control.

Seeing your future

The future. You know there is one. And you have control over what it will be. This time next year you'll be able to look back and see that stuff happened. It might not be great stuff. It might also be amazing stuff. But it's guaranteed that you won't be in this same situation. Do you have a vision of your future?

Is there an ideal future you'd like to see happen? If you had to write down your perfect future, what would it be? Each step we take now is a step into the future.

Visualization

Visualizing the future can be hard if you are not in the right head space. The first time a coach suggested I created a vision board it was not the right moment. I wrote on a piece of paper 'pay bills, eat food', because things were getting tough. The idea of looking at holidays in Barbados felt like a distant memory, not something I should be thinking about right then. In fact, I remember feeling miserable thinking about it. In the past, when I was earning good money, I remember being able to dream anything was possible. I felt like I was in a slipstream; all I needed to do was keep going and I could achieve anything. The daily tasks of signing on, applying for jobs I didn't want, getting rejected from jobs I did want, had made dreaming hard. It all felt more like survival than thriving. Living from day to day, hoping something might come up.

Hope will give you the strength to take a leap into thinking about possibilities, and that is where you can start creating your future. 'Fed up' is just a temporary feeling.

One day you'll get bored of feeling that way and you'll say 'let's do this'. When that happens, when ideas start to come, you can then start to dream, you can then start to think of the consequences of dreaming . . . and visualize the possibilities and what the future could look like if you dream big.

Start a new fashion business . . . consequence – travel the world, attend Paris Fashion Week, get Kate Moss to model first designs, be featured in *Tatler* . . .

If you think that sounds far-fetched look up the story of Molly Gunn's Selfish Mother web platform and The FMLY store. Molly launched her MOTHER T-shirt in 2014 and has since gone on to raise over £1 million for charity.

The future is coming. You can't avoid it but you can shape it. You have a say in what it will look like.

Your Life Dashboard

As you start to ask questions about why you do what you do and who you are, your answers and thoughts will naturally broaden into more than just work. Work and life are becoming ever more interconnected. So, while you are working through pondering what to do next in your career, life stuff is going to crop up. This is where a life coach comes in and says, 'Hello, where shall I sit?' But before you sign up to their life-changing programme, take a mini tour around your current life dashboard and tune into what's going on first.

Some life coaches use a 'wheel of life' to talk around all the parts of your world. It's a simple place to start to think about how you feel, what you focus on, what you neglect, where you want to focus.

Start to understand where your life dashboard is now, where you want it to be, and use it to help navigate your way there. It will show you what is important in your life, where you are focusing right now and where you want to focus.

The life dashboard has six dials:

1. **Wealth and finance**
2. **Health and wellbeing**
3. **Self-growth and learning**
4. **Community and recreation**

5. Family, friends and relationships
6. Career and work

Create your dashboard

Imagine each dial has a setting from 1 to 10 and two needles. One needle shows the current reading, the other needle is showing the aspirational reading, or where you want to be. At any point in your life your dials can change, they can move up and down, stay steady – there is no right or wrong dashboard.

- **Work through each dial.** Write down everything that comes to mind for each section. Write lots of notes as they come to mind. Try not to think about it too much but let the ideas flow.
- **After you've worked through each dial.** Go back and highlight all of the positive scribbles.
- **How many of your scribbles are positive?** Mark each dial between 1 and 10, depending on how much you've highlighted. If all your thoughts are positive, your dial is reading a strong 10. If nothing is highlighted, mark yourself a 1. That is your current reading.
- **What do your readings look like?** What do you want to change?

Note: The aim is not to get all needles to 10 – that is impossible. The aim is to get your needles aligned so you are spending time and focus in the places you want to.

If you need a few prompts to get started, try some of these questions.

1. Wealth and finance

- Do you want to clear debts?
- Do you want to earn more? Why?
- Do you feel in control of money?
- Do you save?
- Do you invest?

2. Health and wellbeing

- Are you healthy?
- Do you exercise?
- Do you eat well?
- Are you a good sleeper?
- Do you feel good right now?
- Do you worry?

3. Self-growth and learning

- Do you spend time on learning new skills?
- Do you read?

- Do you listen to podcasts?
- Do you watch TED talks?
- How do you get new ideas?

4. Community and recreation

- Do you volunteer?
- Do you take part in local events?
- Do you have hobbies?
- Do you have interests you are actively involved with?
- Do you know your neighbours?

5. Family, friends and relationships

- Are you in a happy relationship? Does that matter to you?
- How much time do you spend with family?
- How much time do you spend with friends?
- Do you have a strong support network?
- Do you spend enough time with friends, your partner, your children?

6. Career and work

- Are you happy with your career/specialism?
- Do you have work goals you'd like to achieve?

- What kind of organizations do you admire or would like to work for?
- What qualities do you look for in a manager?
- What type of work are you good at?

When you look at your notes, what stands out for you? Are there big gaps between your current status and what you want it to be?

Being more aware of your life dashboard can help you continually adjust from day to day. It holds the answer to why you feel a bit low on energy some days, why you aren't thriving, why you feel a bit lost. It's the case that where you are putting your energy and where you want to be just aren't aligned.

Here are a few ways you can start to close the gap between where you are spending time and where you want to spend time.

1. What are the things that are taking up most of your time? What things can you start doing to bring you closer to your goal – list three small actions you can start to take tomorrow.
2. Are there some things that you can stop doing? They are no longer aligned, you do them because you think you have to.
3. Are there things you can keep doing but in a different way?

List three reasons why you are not more aligned. How can you flip these into reasons that would mean more alignment? The result will be that you are spending more time doing the things you want to.

Your Priority List

Your life dashboard should help you map out where you are at the moment and the areas that you want to focus on in order to get where you want to be. It is also a really useful tool to help you build your priority list.

1. Your priority list is going to be the foundation for how you move forward. When you have a clear priority list you will know why you are doing something. It will also help you to understand why you might feel frustrated or out of alignment. Your priorities are the reality of your world at any moment in time. They don't reflect your future, they reflect where you are right now. You should always be clear on your priorities, and check in on them, especially if you are having a bad day.

2. When you think about your future, what is going to make the difference to you? How big is the gap between where you are now and your future goals? Your first step to bridge that gap is to be clear about your priorities.

3. Your priority list will help you make decisions and guide you towards your goals. Here are some things you might put on your list:
   - Home by 6 p.m. every day
   - Commute time maximum forty-five minutes

- Never miss children's sports day
- Go to the gym three times a week
- Minimum monthly earnings £7,000

You will always have a number 1 priority. It will always be the thing that you put before anything else. When people say 'I don't have time' they really mean 'I'm not prioritizing that right now'.

If you need to earn money quickly to pay bills then that is your number 1 priority. So you put more energy into this, and even if the job you are doing to bring in money isn't ideal you'll know why you are doing it. So, now you know it's your priority you don't need to waste energy on feeling down about it – you know why you are doing it. You know it's not for ever. You know that your priorities will change and that's what you are working towards.

In your notebook, write down your priority list. This is going to help you make decisions. You'll be clear on the things you will not compromise on when looking for your next job or your next move. Anything you do have to compromise on then is not a priority – check in with what's driving your decision to compromise and be clear with yourself about what you are prioritizing and why.

Get Out of Your Comfort Zone

We all have a comfort zone. A zone that includes all the things that are familiar to us, the reasons we do things, the place where we feel safe, the things that are reliable for us. Being in the comfort zone is nice. It's familiar, it's safe, it's reliable. But is it? Being in your comfort zone is just that, comfortable. It's not the place where change happens. And being in your comfort zone might be the very thing stopping you from growing and moving on. It is not the same as being fulfilled. Sometimes familiarity, safety and reliability are a deception. While routine can help you know what your days will bring, it cannot guarantee satisfaction and happiness.

When you get made redundant, you are thrown from your comfort zone. You don't know what you want next so you apply for jobs that match what you do already. A mixture of panic, uncertainty and reassurance means that the line of least resistance is to apply for what you know. But is that what you want? Do you want to stick with what you know, stay in your comfort zone and get a similar role to what you had? That's OK if you do – but do it because you want to.

The zone next door to your comfort zone is your stretch zone, where you dare to learn, step up to grow, start to do something different. When you get the right support and resources behind you to give you a chance of success. Stretch will feel uncomfortable but for the right reasons; you'll experience new things, you'll get satisfaction through growing. This is your chance to decide if losing your job is your chance to do something different, create a new stretch zone, or stay comfortable. Stick, twist, bust. There are no right or wrong decisions. There are just decisions that you own.

A gentle word of warning about the stress zone

So far, I've been encouraging you into your stretch zone. Even if it's just to explore possibilities and think about 'what if'. The stretch zone is a magic place. But it comes with a health warning. If you push yourself too hard you put pressure on yourself, if you take on too much, if you stretch without the right support, you will quickly move into the stress zone. The stress zone is your warning that you aren't supporting yourself, you aren't helping yourself, you aren't getting the magical benefit of growth. You need to take a step back. If you are in an unfamiliar place, trying to do something new, living in uncertainty, the line between stretch and stress is a thin one. Tune in. Make sure you are looking after yourself. Ask for help. Keep your stretch zone healthy.

Work on your stretch zone

Your aim is to keep yourself in the stretch zone, where you will experience a healthy amount of challenge, a feeling of ambition and progress, combined with a feeling of control and satisfaction. When you open up, things will present themselves to you. You can then work on turning them into opportunities or letting go and moving on. When you are in stretch you are growing. When you are in stress you are stalling. When you are in comfort you feel certain

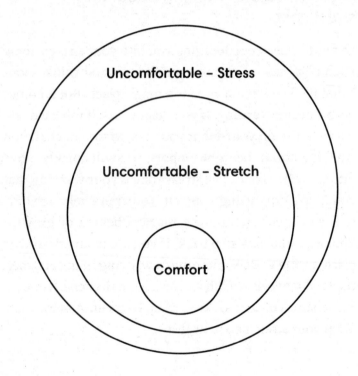

and safe. Be aware of the things that occupy your zone. Are they giving you comfort, stretch or stress? Tune in and manage your zones.

CASE STUDY – Shakil

'Stepping away from decades of work is an invaluable chance to start afresh. When I swapped the world of work for pastures new in the consultancy space I took a leap of faith into an unknown zone, challenging and stretching myself to grow and learn. In truth, the first twelve months felt long and dragged on, while in other ways they passed in the blink of an eye. I'd been an employee for thirty years and had known nothing but employed work since I was eighteen. It is often said work gives you purpose, and there is without doubt some truth in that. Every morning of every working day I knew I had somewhere to go, a role to play, some value to add. I would have people looking to me to lead, to develop solutions and to bring people together around a shared organizational issue. I had my own air-conditioned office with a leather chair, I had a team of colleagues, some of whom I'd worked with for years and built meaningful relationships with. The projects, the scope, the scale and people all changed during these thirty years but the one constant was a sense that I mattered in the workplace and had a contribution to make. As I became more senior, my workload grew and increasingly I became a person with a title. Work became a distraction from life itself. So when I was made redundant it was more than losing my job. It felt like I'd lost my identity. I was out of my comfort zone, out of the my known operating zone, into unknown territory.

'Taking away that job title forced me to ask the question – who does that leave? I am so much more than my title, my qualification, my experience and competence, which typically in the employment market is primarily what is being assessed. I was made redundant after thirty years at the same company. This meant the workload was taken away and suddenly I could breathe again. While I may have lost my role, I had now begun to find myself, asking myself those tough questions about my purpose in life, my personal vision, my mission and my values. My entire identity was wrapped up in the job in which I'd spent more time as an adult than anywhere else, including my home. On my last day, the sense of loss, knowing my life was about to change for ever, was mixed with an enormous relief, I was finally free. Since then, like any loss or bereavement, there are times I have longed to turn back the clock and run into my comfort zone but the adventure of what lies ahead also calls to me. I can only grow and reach my true potential if I move into a zone that stretches and challenges me – and at times makes me feel hugely uncomfortable. I know the leap into the unknown was what I needed to do.'

Shakil is now a HR consultant and speaker.

You are Never Too Old

If you have been made redundant towards the end of your career and are concerned that you are too old to do anything new, to think differently or adapt, you are wrong! Age is just a number. People want to work with people. Employers want diversity in their teams and their organizations. They are looking for attitude, connection and experience. They want people who are curious, eager to adapt and learn and use their curiosity mindset. Regardless of your age, here are some indications that you're still in the game. The more ticks on this list, the more in the game you still are:

- ✔ You are curious and want to hear about new things.
- ✔ You believe in 'always learning' and you believe you can always improve.
- ✔ You are open to new ideas.
- ✔ You don't judge.
- ✔ You embrace new technology.
- ✔ You find new friends, new circles, new connections.
- ✔ You start new hobbies and interests.
- ✔ You don't live by 'that's just the way I do things'.

Your experience is of value to someone. You can use your experience to help others. You can use your experience to help you do something completely different. You've been successful before, you can draw on that experience again.

Wobbles and Triggers

Just as you start feeling better and are getting yourself into a good place – bang! You see on LinkedIn that Judy has landed her job, a job you would love to do, and now she is in the desirable position of earning again, and banking the redundancy pay. The ultimate dream! Suddenly the whirlpool starts to turn and drag you down, back into the darkness of uncertainty and self-sorrow. It's not fair. Lucky her. Why not you? There's an easy way to deal with this. Delete Judy.

Do not get distracted by what others are doing. This is your time. Not theirs. And you don't know the full story. Judy might still be totally miserable. That job might be awful. Or she might be having a great time. It doesn't really matter. It's totally irrelevant to what you are doing right now. When you are feeling fed up, every now and then you will get triggered. There's no science or logic to when a trigger will come along and for everyone it is different.

There was one day I was close to tears because I was trying to create a password. The automated password creator popped up on screen and announced, 'Your password is weak'. It was the final trigger that day. I read it as if my life was talking to me. 'Bit weak,' it says. 'Could try harder,' it says. 'Reject,' it says. (It said none of those things.) I remember thinking, *Even my password is weak*, sniff. *Pass me the gin. That doesn't think I'm weak.*

You are going through an uncertain time, things get sensitive. Emotions get triggered. Wobble days are going to happen. Have a wobble-day plan – the music you play, the film you watch, the walk you take, the person you talk to. And then wobble over it and start again tomorrow.

The 3 a.m. Awake Club

Wobble days are one thing, but wobble nights? They are a whole different ball game. You wake up at 3 a.m. Your whole life is crashing around you. You worry. You can't see a way through. You feel despair.

You can't resist picking up your phone and googling job searches. You click refresh on emails, in case you've missed one from a recruiter. You scroll through Facebook. Look at all those happy people having holidays and buying cars and having fun with their families. The whole world is sleeping. They've abandoned you here, alone with your thoughts. When will this end? When will you feel normal again?

The 3 a.m. Awake Club's five rules to make you feel better

- **Rule 1: You are not alone.** It's estimated that 62 per cent of the population has sleep problems.
- **Rule 2: Find your routine.** Sleep specialist Dr Wendy Troxel says in one of her TED talks, 'Our brains learn by association. To sleep well you want your brain to have a strong learned association between the bed and sleep.' She advises you stick to a routine with the same bedtime every evening and with your alarm set

for the same time every morning, including weekends.

- **Rule 3: Make the most of your sleep cycle.** Some of us are night owls, some of us are morning larks. We are all working on twenty-four-hour body cycles. Society has decided that it favours the morning lark but if you are a night owl, make the most of the time that you're awake while everyone else is asleep.
- **Rule 4: Get scribbling.** If your thoughts are going round and round in your head, get scribbling. It might be an opportunity to turn your anxieties into something productive.
- **Rule 5: Get mindful.** If you have been awake for more than twenty minutes, get up. Try listening to some guided meditation. If you've never tried meditation before now is a great time to start. Suspend judgement and see what happens. YouTube is full of sleep meditations and there are lots of free apps. Give it a go.

Sleepless nights are caused by anxiety and worry. Tell your 3 a.m. self that it's OK, there is nothing you can do right there and then. Breathe into the night, read, write, let go of worry noise in your head. It's going to be OK. A day is starting with fresh opportunity.

Digital Detox

Did you know how much your work helped you stay away from your phone, or to be precise, from scrolling on your phone? Now, without work getting in the way, you are free to be attached to your phone every hour of the day and night. Sure, you have a very good excuse because you need to be on your phone all the time to take advantage of any opportunities that might arise. So, it's essential you are always 'on' – right?

Social media can be friend or foe. The problem with having time on your hands is you also usually have a smartphone in your hands too. If you are searching for what will happen next – new job, new career, course application – it can become your nemesis as well as your friend. You get hooked on waiting for the ping, you don't want to miss that opportunity, the refresh button is pressed every ten minutes – just in case. It can become very unhealthy. Even though your smartphone may be your lifeline at the moment you need to monitor how much you use it and try a detox here and there, for the sake of your sanity.

In his book *Digital Minimalism* Cal Newport advocates using technology on a small number of activities that actively serve you and benefit your needs. Structuring your days so you only focus your job search and work opportunities in the morning, then switching off your devices to digital detox every afternoon, could be one way to maintain a healthy relationship with your technology. If that sounds hard, try one day a week at first, or one hour a day, then two, then three . . .

You know you are overdosing on social media when . . .

- The first thing you do when you wake up is reach for your phone.
- You only know what the weather is like from the BBC weather app.
- You are a 'Like' hoarder.
- You miss your train stop because you were swiping and are now two hours out from your destination.
- You know everything about *Bake Off* from Twitter but you've never actually watched the programme.

Time away from social media

If completely avoiding your devices is too much of a challenge while you're looking for work, limiting your time on social media may be a good alternative way to remain sane. Social media can help you connect, network, get your message out there, find new opportunities. But too much time spent scrolling can limit your productivity.

Here are some tips to manage your time on social media

- **Allocate time for social-media scrolling.** You can limit your time on certain apps on your phone.
- **Leave your phone downstairs when you go up to bed.** That way you won't be reaching for your phone during your 3 a.m. freak-out.
- **Unsubscribe.** Get rid of groups, pages, newsletters and apps that you haven't used for a while.
- **Be a producer not a consumer.** Find the groups that do the work for you. Post about your progress. Make social media work for you.

It's important to manage the amount of time you spend online. Throughout this book I urge you to make notes in a journal. You and your journal should be spending just as much time together as you and your smartphone. Monitor your digital usage and take this as an opportunity to use it less, in a more intentional way.

Coming Out of Stuck

As you spend more time thinking about you, who you are, seeing yourself in a different way, wishes will start to become ideas. You can begin to see things from a different perspective, with hope and optimism. You know there are many possibilities for you.

- Capture where you are right now.
- What are those ideas that have been repeating in your mind?
- If you had the opportunity right now, what would be your ideal scenario?
- What do you feel are the things stopping you?

You will have big bursts of energy and periods of despair, your moments of *Oh* and moments of *Oh no!* It's all normal. Embrace it. It's time to start something new.

Stuck top tip – align your priorities and your actions

Be clear what your priorities are, and why. Challenge yourself. Where are you focusing your time, your efforts and your energy? Are your priorities aligned with where you want to be, what you want to do? If you aren't taking small actions, creating small steps that are contributing towards your goals, then you won't be any closer to achieving them. Constantly check in with your priorities.

Part 3

Slow,
Slow, Go

As you leave your stuck phase, your internal voices will start to alternate between *This is exciting* and *You can't do it*. Or *This could work* and *You don't have the skills*. Or *This is a brilliant idea* and *You could never pull it off*. It's exhausting. But possible.

This internal narrative is normal. It's your way of trying to protect yourself. Keep moving yourself through to action. If you've been letting your ideas roam free then it's time to start making some decisions. Do you have a notebook full of ideas? A head full of dreams? What questions do you need answered? What decisions do you need to make?

And now it's not so much about having ideas, as the question of where to start. Are you getting clearer on what your priorities are, what you'd really like to happen next? What are you going to do? Stick, twist or bust?

As ideas and possibilities start to flow, processing how all this could happen in reality can become unnerving. You've gone from feeling shocked, to stuck for ideas, to not knowing what to do next. As we've already discussed. Being 'stuck' is part of ongoing life. It never goes away. It's our way of telling ourselves we need to change something or solve something. It's a good thing to feel stuck. It means you are ready to explore. Slowing down and taking stock is part of the process. After spending time on yourself and all that thinking, and then the excitement of generating ideas, your mind will be trying to fight you. It still wants to protect you.

'Slow, Slow, Go' is about checking where you are at, being clear on your why, being confident that you are making the right decision then lining up all that energy to 'go'. Go with purpose and intent so that results happen quicker than continuing to meander along with a half-hearted idea.

Being Clear on Your Why

Knowing your why – why you want to do something, why you are doing something – is the foundation to making good, impactful decisions. The first part of slowing down is to clarify your why so that you can make good decisions.

In 'Stuck', we explored lots of whats – what do you want to do, what are the possibilities, what are your opinions?

In this part of the book we now ask why? Why do you want to do this?

In his book *Start with Why*, Simon Sinek talks about why the why is so important: 'Very few people can articulate why they do what they do. By Why I mean your purpose, cause, belief. Why do you get up in the morning? Why should anyone else care? People don't buy what you do, they buy why you do it.'

This is vital because whatever decision you make – whether to stick, twist or bust – you'll need to 'sell' yourself in some way: at an interview, through your CV, in your marketing, at a pitch. If you are clear on your why this makes decisions easier, and it helps people to understand and connect with you.

Your why is also strongly linked to your values. When you know your values, and live by them, that's when you become aligned not just to what you say you do, but also

'Some people are in a position to trade the security of a regular salary in order to pursue a passion, many simply can't . . . But following the money and following your heart don't have to be mutually exclusive. By shifting the lens in which you view what you are doing now, you can profoundly shift your experience of it.'

Margie Warrell, Stop Playing Safe

to how you do it. When you understand your values and live by them you'll attract opportunities that more closely fit your ideal scenario.

In *The Squiggly Career*, Sarah Ellis and Helen Tupper talk through an exercise, summarized below, that helps you start to understand your values:

1. **Reflecting** – We've done some of this already, but here capture your career highs and lows noting what has gone well, and what was happening when things weren't great.
2. **Spotting** – Ask yourself what's important. This might link to your priority list, but this also might be more about behaviours and attitudes. What is important to you about the people you work with, work for and the environment you work in.
3. **Scanning** – Make a list of words to scan and choose the ones that jump out. For this exercise just make a list of words that spring to mind when you are asked, 'What behaviours and attitudes are important to you?' e.g. loyalty, freedom, fun, achievement, success, etc. and pick the five most important to you.
4. **Prioritizing** – This is where you rank the values you've captured from the exercises above. What is the most important value to you? Rank your top five. And note why they are important.

From this simple exercise you can start to form a view of not just what your priorities are, but what is important when it comes to how and why you do something.

Knowing your 'why' might feel overwhelming, like you have to have some huge grand purpose to save the world, but it's not about that. Your why is what gives you energy, it's where your passion lies, it's where you feel you contribute.

Five questions you can ask yourself to help you find your why

1. What are the things that bother you and that you want to change in life?
2. What do people say about you, believe about you, see in you?
3. What are the things that bring you happiness and fulfilment?
4. What are your values and the things that matter when it comes to how you do something?
5. Where do your energy surges and drive come from?

Your why is your greater purpose. It can be a macro-driven world-changing mission, or it can be a micro-driven personal-centred focus – it doesn't matter what size, what matters is that it matters to you.

Slow down and be clear on your why.

'When your vision for your life is powered by meaning, you develop superhero strength to step out, be seen and save your own day.'

Jessica Huie, Purpose

Analysis Paralysis

So you might be getting clear on your why, but the whats . . . the whats are many. What do you want to do? So many ideas, so many decisions to make – or are there?

This is when you overthink your decisions to such an extent that you never move on or take action. You become so overwhelmed you do nothing. We don't want that. You have come so far. To give up before you've even started is not a possibility. There is a happy medium between using your clear-headed thinking and reaching analysis paralysis.

Here are some tips to get you slowly moving in the right direction:

- Be clear on your priority list. You might want to stick it to a wall where you can see it every day. It will keep your mind focused on what you're working towards.
- Don't force things. If you're doing something for the sake of it or because you think you should, pause. This is more than likely a waste of energy that could be better spent elsewhere.
- Keep asking questions. Follow up on leads. Reach out to people on LinkedIn.
- Limit yourself to a few actions a day.

- Be intentional about why you are doing things but do them without expectation. Just let things flow.

Right now it's about keeping things simple. You don't have to have all the answers, you don't need everything all worked out, you don't require a detailed plan of action. Tune into what your intuition tells you to do and move away from overthinking and overanalysing.

Decisions, Decisions

Time to decide. Were you even aware that you had decisions to make? You were unexpectedly put in this situation of being out of work. Up to that point you had other things on your mind. Other things were getting your attention. And now you are having to decide what to do next. How good are you at making decisions?

Do decisions scare you? Is the prospect of having to decide what to do next filling you with dread? Are there too many forks in the road? If this is sounding familiar, rest assured. I'm going to show you how you can always make the right decision at the right time.

You can only make good decisions if you maintain sufficient mental energy. Once this energy starts to get low, self-control becomes impaired, leading to 'decision fatigue' – a term coined by Roy Baumeister, a psychologist known for a wide range of work on the self, social rejection, motivation and aggression, to explain the decline in the quality of our decision making when we make a large number of decisions consecutively.

Understanding the psychological principle of decision fatigue can help you make positive changes to your lifestyle so you can save your mental energy and willpower for the most important decisions.

Baumeister explains that things cannot be achieved with willpower alone. In the next few pages we explore how breaking things down into small steps can overcome willpower fatigue. But what about decision making? Well, it's a similar idea. Reducing the amount of things you have to make a decision on frees up time and energy. Decision fatigue explains why you may start to look for shortcuts in your decision making throughout the day. You might even decide to give up and do nothing when you are faced with a decision.

This state of decision making routinely warps your judgement. While most people are unaware of it, decision fatigue can have a lot of lasting consequences.

Decidophobia

Did you know there is an actual fear of making decisions? It must be true because I read it on the internet. Decidophobia, like most phobias, stems from a subconscious overprotection mechanism. It may be rooted in a person's fear of being responsible for others as well as a generalized fear of failure.

Do you know how you make decisions?

Every decision you take results from a battle in your mind – a battle between intuition and logic. The intuitive part of your mind is a lot more powerful than you might think. Most of us like to believe that we are capable of making rational decisions. We may at times rely on our gut instinct, but if necessary we can call on our powers of reason to arrive at a logical decision. We like to think that our beliefs, judgements and opinions are based on solid reasoning. But are they? Slowing down your thinking and your decision making and concentrating on how you are forming thoughts and deciding what to do will give you a more impactful outcome when it comes to making your move.

CASE STUDY – Alison

'In a blind panic, the feeling [I needed] to do something and make decisions and sort this situation out spun me in a thousand directions. I felt like I was lost at sea, thrashing my arms, hoping someone would throw a life jacket and give me a way out. I splashed so much I couldn't think clearly or see opportunities. I needed some calm, lapping water to gather my thoughts and work out a plan of where to head next. I started to do too many things all at the same time. I wasn't sure what I really wanted. I got over-whelmed, I was overthinking, trying too hard, not sure where I was going with it all. I had lots of ideas. That wasn't the issue. I even had a few job opportunities on the table. But it all felt in a muddle and I just couldn't grab the thing I really needed. A bit like losing your house keys in your bag, so much stuff in there, but the thing you need you can never find! I thought because I was keeping myself busy with stuff I was making progress. However, too much stuff, too much going on, is unproductive. I stopped. I thought about the few things that really mattered to me. I got focused and things began to change.'

How to make better decisions

A morning routine can help you think more clearly. Start your day with a ritual. That may be a nice cup of coffee and a shower or fifteen minutes of meditation. (It's definitely not fifteen minutes of scrolling on your smart-phone.) You don't have to wake up at 5 a.m. for a gym session. Tailor your routine to suit you. It will help kick-start your day and put you in the right frame of mind to take on some tricky decisions.

- Make important decisions in the morning. There is a reason why we say 'let's sleep on it'. Your mind is the clearest during the morning because you're not yet worn out from the day's activities. You haven't been faced with all those decisions yet, and you are able to stop and think about your situation. After your morning ritual, schedule in time to pause, ponder and decide.
- Don't make decisions when you're hungry or tired. It may sound obvious, but being out of sorts can negatively impact your decision making.
- Reduce distractions around you when you're making decisions. Set aside some specific time with nothing else around. You might want to turn your phone off and log off your social media.
- Change your location. If you're not able to create a distraction-free space at home, try somewhere else. Go for a swim, a run or a walk; it will get the ideas flowing and help you reach a decision.
- Tune into your gut instinct. You don't need to have lots of data, research, facts; sometimes just

tuning into what you would do if put on the spot there and then will give you the answer. A great trick to help you tune into your gut to is flip a coin to make a (non-binding) decision. When the coin lands how do you feel about which way it landed? Relieved? Concerned?

- Focus on the few things that will help you achieve your goals. If you want to work closer to home, stop applying for jobs with long commutes. If you want to work for an organization that is closer to your values, stop being lured into applying for jobs with a big salary. Use your priority list to be clear on what is influencing your actions.
- Be clear on the pros and cons on either side of the decision. Write down the two sides of the argument, wearing both hats – what's the worst that can happen, what's the best that can happen?

Do not be afraid of making a decision. Decisions are right when you make them. Things can change if and when they have to. Know why you are doing something and know you can always make changes if things don't feel right. Don't fear the decision.

Your Getting Stuff Done List

Once you start gaining momentum, your to-do list will get busy. You'll start getting lots of things to do, people to see, webinars to watch, newsletters to sign up to.

You'll wonder how you'll ever have time to fit in work again.

You'll feel like you have to do everything so that you don't miss opportunities. But you don't have to do *everything*. Be ruthless with your list. You'll get more stuff done the fewer things you have on it. What does your to-do list look like? Your real to-do list? Do you really need to do all the things on it?

Make a list of everything going on right now. Everything. Even those jobs you keep putting off but that linger in the back of your mind. Now choose three things you will definitely not be doing this week. Cross them off. Next choose three things you will absolutely focus on achieving this week. The three things you choose should be those that will help you move furthest towards your goals. Put everything else on hold.

When you start owning your list it becomes less need, more want. When you *want* to do the things on your list it becomes easier. If you have a big list of things you feel like you *need* to do that just makes the task even harder. Slowing down to identify a few things that you know you can achieve will keep you going.

If you have identified changes you want to make, the next step is to identify things you can do to move forward. Maybe the changes you want are big, huge, scary – impossible. Of course, they are not impossible, but they need to be broken down. Even minor changes – small steps, different perspectives, different priorities – still need thought and attention. Avoid 'I will do it tomorrow' syndrome creeping in by finding small things to do that are achievable. Your getting-stuff-done list needs to be short, achievable and something you look forward to working on.

Procrastination

We all do it. One moment, we are looking at our to-do list thinking about how urgent it all seems and the next we're alphabetizing our spice shelf, reading an old magazine retrieved from under the sofa or spending five hours creating an elaborate spreadsheet to plan how we are going to start doing said to-do list. Procrastination isn't about laziness, it's a diversion our brain uses when we are finding our workload overwhelming.

Tim Herrera, co-author of *Smarter Living*, writes: 'Our brains tend to prioritize immediate satisfaction over long-term rewards. A study found that subjects were more likely to perform urgent, smaller tasks with a deadline than more important tasks without an immediate time constraint, even if the option to perform the urgent task is objectively worse than performing the larger one.'

We prefer urgent tasks with shorter deadlines over important tasks with larger outcomes, because important tasks are usually harder and further away from goal completion. We are wired to search for the immediate hit. So are you putting things off? Finding distractions? Staying safe rather than making those bold decisions?

If you have some big ideas, but you are thinking the time isn't right – you'll do it when x happens, you'll do it when y is in place – ask yourself are these reasons real, or are you finding excuses?

'To all of my procrastinators out there, I offer an explanation: Your brain is working against you, and it's because of a phenomenon called the urgency effect.'

Tim Herrera

The Eisenhower Grid

There is a great tool to help you clarify what you should be focusing on.

	URGENT	NOT URGENT
IMPORTANT	**DO** *Do it now* Write article for today	**DECIDE** *Schedule a time to do it* Exercising Calling family and friends Researching articles Long-term biz strategy
NOT IMPORTANT	**DELEGATE** *Who can do it for you?* Scheduling interviews Booking flights Approving comments Answering certain emails Sharing articles	**DELETE** *Eliminate it* Watching television Checking social media Sorting through junk mail

'What is important is seldom urgent and what is urgent is seldom important.'

Dwight Eisenhower,
34th President of the United States

Stephen Covey talks about the Eisenhower decision principle in *The 7 Habits of Highly Effective People*. He creates a matrix to help decide what's important and not important and what's urgent and not urgent.

Go through your tasks on your to-do list and place them in one of the four boxes. It should help you prioritize what to do when. What are the most important things to you right now? List everything you have in order – the things closest to your priority list at the top, things not contributing at the bottom, then sort depending on time urgency. Then be disciplined; either Do it, Delete it, Decide whether to do it or Delegate – or find another way to do it.

If you need time to work through your lists, schedule in Do it time, Delete it time, Decide time and Delegate time during the day. Stick to the time slots. It's easy to say just do the Do it list, but in reality we all stray a little. So scheduling intended time to stray makes it OK.

Foods and Moods

While you are slowing down a little, it's a good time to check whether you are looking after yourself.

You should take care of yourself before you have to. Why does it take an illness (or someone else's illness) for us to decide to take a look at our health? The simple answer is that it doesn't come naturally to most of us. Being out of work, spending time at home, can mean the temptation of the biscuit tin and the cup of tea to fill in time, the idle time in the house. And what about all those catch-up coffees and cake? Now I need to confess here that the idea for this book was created during a regular coffee-and-cake morning (which often ended at 3 p.m.), so I know all about the role food starts to play in filling time when you are looking for your next move. My cake buddy, Helen, and I sorted the world out during those meet-ups across the Wiltshire countryside – but I don't think our waistlines thanked us for it!

What I had to consciously work hard on was creating more time for wellness and self-care!

Those Hobnobs might feel like your friend, especially when you've just received your fifth rejection email of the day, but those Hobnobs are not your friend! It's the perfect time to challenge your wellness.

No more excuses for not getting exercise because you are too busy. No more ready meals because they fit into your hectic lifestyle. If you are feeling low or lacking energy, what you are eating could be contributing. This is a quick checklist, but if you're serious about your well-being, find a programme to follow and start to make changes now. Mind.org.uk/food has great advice to start you thinking about what you are eating and helping you become more aware of how it may be affecting you. You can also find specialist practitioners who are able to give you advice and support on freelancedietitian.org or bant.org.uk. Simple things like introducing more fresh food and less processed food, or checking labels for artificial sweeteners, preservatives and colourings can have a big impact. And of course, drinking lots of water!

Take on your health and wellness. You need to be at peak performance to make the best of any opportunities that come along. Just because you aren't at the office and finding natural breaks to take in water (what do you mean you never drunk water at work?) doesn't mean you don't need it. Make sure you still get your five glasses a day. And no, that doesn't include coffee and tea.

The Power of Meditation and Mindfulness

While we are talking wellness, let's talk meditation and mindfulness. I've already mentioned the power of pausing, taking time out, slowing down, being still. It's the ultimate tool in your kit to be more productive. Meditation and mindfulness can change the game for you. I don't profess to be an expert but I did take it up when I was feeling low, and it helped me rest and gain perspective. There are plenty of apps, mini courses and videos online.

Mindfulness and meditation focus on remaining present in any moment. They help to draw your attention away from any concerns you have about the future or any difficulties you've been having in the past. Together, they create a set of disciplines that bring you into your body and help you focus on your surroundings and observe your thoughts in a more detached way.

You might want to start with mindfulness, to ease you in. Mindfulness is a form of meditation whereby you bring your mind to the one thing you are focusing on, whether that's listening to Beethoven or eating a sandwich. Mindfulness is an awareness of your life, thoughts, feelings, emotions, body – senses, surroundings, people – and focusing on one thing at a time. Mindful meditation is either a guided meditation (e.g. breathing, a body scan), a sitting meditation or a visualization (ocean, lake or mountain meditation). It can also take the form of informal meditation when you are walking, eating, listening or talking, for example, which focuses the mind on what you are doing, noticing when your mind has wandered and then bringing it back to the matter at hand. Mindfulness and meditation can have a life-changing impact. People use them to overcome worries, stress, illness, even to solve problems.

A calmer and clearer mind, lowered anxiety and anger levels, improved concentration and focus, greater resilience, a greater ability to accept and let stuff go . . . and balance. Other benefits are an improved relationship with food; a greater awareness of our physical wellbeing, so aiding pain relief; a strengthened immune system; and better quality of sleep. It can also enhance your happiness and your connection with others, help you to be less judgemental, and encourage more forgiveness, kindness and compassion both to others and, importantly, to yourself. Why wouldn't you give it a go?

It's all about being conscious of breathing. Taking a breath. A deep breath will help you relax, it will help you have hope, it will give you some space. When you are conscious of your breathing you can feel more in control of your life. Before an interview, before you make a phone call, before you pitch an idea – breathe. Try small things to get instant benefit. Daily practice can be encouraged by setting your alarm or pinning up notes around your home to remind you to stop what you are doing, breathe deeply and check in with your body.

You Have to Laugh

It feels like we've spent a lot of time with lists and thinking and prioritizing. So as a bit of time out, and in the spirit of 'Slow, Slow, Go', let's talk about laughing. When was the last time you laughed? Why were you laughing? Are you smiling now just thinking about it? Isn't it just the best feeling when you laugh? Spontaneous, uncontrollable laughter? You can laugh at yourself. That's OK. You don't have to get embarrassed over those little things that happen to you. Now I'm not saying we should all become comedians, but finding humour and not humiliation or embarrassment could really help us get through the day sometimes. Choose laughter instead of upset every time.

When you laugh, your muscles contract, which increases blood flow, stimulating the heart and lungs and releasing endorphins. This helps you relax and feel better almost instantly. That moment when you get back in your car after a bizarre meeting or interview and you sit there and think, 'Did that just happen?' At times like those you have a choice. You can get a bit cross. 'What a waste of time! What a dick! What a load of rubbish!' – or you can smile. You can think, 'What a lucky escape. How funny!' Seeing the humour can help build resilience. The way you bounce back from the bad things that happen to you has a huge impact on how quickly you can move on. Resilience is the ability to see failure as a natural

'The healthiest response to life is laughter.'

Deepak Chopra

precursor to success. The ability to acknowledge mistakes without anger or frustration plays an important role in building resilience. Laughing at mistakes allows us to acknowledge that they're just part of being human.

Creating time for laughter is a proven stress relief

If you are feeling low, watching your favourite funny film, or your favourite comedy DVD (dust off that old DVD player in the attic . . . or just download on Netflix!) can have a significant instant uplift on your day. You can even join laughter clubs and laughter yoga – search online for your local class. What's not to like?

Taking time out to laugh is not to be underrated. You might be going through a tough time. But you can laugh. And your day will instantly improve.

It's Time to Go!

So we've paused, we've slowed down, we've got clarity, we've got confidence in the decisions we make, we know our why. We are ready to go. It's time to take action.

Top tip to slowing down

By now I hope you've got a journal full of scribbled notes, ideas, moments of *Oh* and dreams ready to leap into life. If you haven't, do it now. Your journal needs to be chock full of all sorts by the time you finish this book.

List your moments of *Oh* that stand out for you so far. Think about what they mean for you. These will be important as you develop your ideas and actions.

So – what do you want to do?

Why do you want to do it?

Let's go . . . let's now explore how you are going to do it . . .

Let's do this.

Part 4

Unstuck

Let's go. Being unstuck is the feeling you get when you are ready to go, when you are moving on and have clear purpose. That feeling. Remember it. It's when all your moments of *Oh* start coming together.

Enjoy this part. Becoming unstuck is about being intentional. It's about absolute focus on what you want to achieve and taking actions that move you closer to achieving it.

In this section we are going to develop a plan that will help you achieve your goal, whether it's stick, twist or bust – or a hybrid of stick first but with the aim to bust later.

Your life might start to feel exciting, as though things might actually happen. Redundancy can be a gift. It might not feel that way at the time, but if you catch it, use it, make it work for you then it can be a life-changing experience rather than just a job change. It can help you address far more areas of your life than just what you do for a living. So, what are you going to do? Stick, twist or bust? When you begin to feel 'unstuck' and ideas start to flow, you'll be thinking about 'how'. How am I going to start this? How is this going to work? How will this pan out? Your challenge now is to hold your nerve.

Plan your success. Keep in control. Keep focused. Go mad for Post-it notes. (Actually, don't do that; it's not great for the environment and you'll get buried in neon paper. Get a whiteboard instead.) This is now Operation Smash It.

'Planning is bringing the future into the present so you can do something about it now.'

Alan Lakein

Kate Southerby is a confidence coach. I asked her how it felt to be unstuck:

'It's like you're in the middle of a forest and you're lost,' she said. 'You have four paths ahead of you, but you don't know which one will take you to where you want to go. But, you have to make a decision to take one of them, you can't remain stuck in the forest. It might not end up being the right path to take for the long term, you may even need to head back to that central spot again, but you can't stay stuck in the middle of that forest.

'Any kind of move is a good move. Often one path is actually connected to another path once you step down it. Taking any kind of action is helpful to you. It moves your brain into or towards a reward state. The process and confidence of stepping onto the path is the hardest part. Of making the choice based on what feels right for you at that time.'

To become unstuck you need to work on three areas:

- Your plan.
- Your story.
- Your tribe.

Your Plan

We are going to create a simple plan of objectives and actions that will avoid your brain expending unnecessary energy on thinking and remembering what you are doing and why, and instead focus on how you are going to do it.

A simple plan might look like this:

- **Objectives** – What am I aiming to do?
- **Purpose** – Why am I doing this?
- **Outcomes** – What do I expect to achieve?
- **Barriers** – What will stop me?
- **Resources** – What resources do I have, and need?
- **Timing** – When will this happen, is there sequencing needed?
- **Interdependencies** – What other things are linked to this goal?

I tried to think of a fancy acronym (are you missing those corporate acronyms yet?) but OPOBRTI are not great letters to play *Countdown* conundrum with! So back to the plan.

Once you have a basic plan outline, you'll be able to expand in more detail.

Your plan will involve you wearing a few different

hats – development, learning and promoting and delivery. You will wear one hat more often than the others depending on what you are doing and what you are trying to do. Let's go back to stick, twist or bust.

If you are aiming to stick, but perhaps upgrade, then your plan will focus on promotion (of yourself) and delivery (pitching at interview). This will help you improve your story, your confidence, your CV and your interview skills.

If you are aiming to twist and go freelance or work as a consultant, then your plan will be focused on development, for example setting up as a sole trader, creating your network, finding your first client.

If you are aiming to bust it and start a new business, or do something completely different that involves retraining, then your plan will be focused on learning; researching the market, finding out about competition/who does it already, learning new skills. Being clear on what you are trying to do, and staying aware of which hat you need to wear when, will help you manage the overwhelm.

When you plan in advance and set yourself goals for the next five years or ninety days, the next month or week, or even the next day, those goals will feel more achievable and less intimidating. You can't do all the things you think you need to do at once. Magic happens when you hold your focus and don't get distracted. If you really want something you have to plan to get it. If opportunities come along that are going to take you off plan, think hard about the value of the distraction versus the value of getting on with the plan.

That is all you need to do for now. Plans are just a sense of knowing what you are doing and why. They don't need to be hard work; they should be fun. They are your quick way to getting what you want.

Your Story

Right now your day might look like this: get up (good so far), make coffee, call a recruiter, talk for thirty minutes about yourself, eat toast, apply for job through Indeed, write about yourself, get dressed, eat a sandwich (spill crumbs in car but not all over interview outfit), go to an interview, talk for two hours about yourself, drive home, speak with another fellow redundantee, talk about yourself for a bit, listen to them talking about themselves for a bit, make coffee, talk to partner about your day of talking about yourself, ask them about their day, they say, 'Yeah, it was all right,' eat, go to bed. There can sometimes be a lot of you talking and thinking about you. And that's really tiring.

Getting to grips with your story, and really knowing and owning it, is going to help manage this fatigue and make you confident when sharing it with the world. You need to own your narrative and sell yourself like never before.

Sell yourself? I mean I'm not suggesting you put yourself up on eBay or Amazon but . . . if you were to put yourself up for sale how would you word the advert? Go on, give it a go.

- Category
- Headline
- Description
- Special features and details

- History
- Batteries included?
- Price

It's a fun exercise to do, and if you have a great imagination it's amazing what you create as your brand. There are probably lots of clever psychological things to be analysed out of how you describe yourself – and as for the price, hands up who put over £1m? But that's not what it's about. It's just a creative way to get you thinking about yourself. And if you find it awkward and uncomfortable then you need to work really hard in this space.

Your story, how you talk about yourself, will really help you move forward. You might not always have to talk about yourself directly but just knowing who you are and why you are doing something, and all the things that make you unique, will give you the confidence to talk about anything.

Writing your story

- **Your why** – Why do you do what you do?
- **Your elevator pitch** – In no more than two minutes, describe what it is you're about.
- **Your expertise** – What are your strengths? What do you naturally excel at? What skills have you developed?

- **Your achievements** – When do you thrive? What is your best performance? Do you respond well to pressure? Do you like working alone or in teams? Are you better on projects?
- **Your passion** – What gets you up in the morning? What lights up your day? What do you enjoy doing?
- **Your background** – What is your history? What is your experience? How did you get to do the things you've done?

Thinking about your story and writing it down will help you

- answer questions in interviews,
- introduce yourself at networking events,
- update your CV,
- pitch your idea,
- sell yourself to clients,
- gain the confidence to put yourself out there.

Writing your story doesn't mean your whole life story, and it doesn't mean a long, beautifully written script. But it is about being clear on the things that matter to you and how you articulate that and make it work for you.

Your Tribe

You need the right people around you; the people who support you, who listen, who get it. If you are starting something new, going bold, the people around you will play a big part in your experience. Creating a tribe who hustle your vibe in the right direction is one of the biggest factors affecting your success. You need your tribe, they will help you along.

Your tribe is not the same thing as your network, friends and family. Your tribe is your vibe. When I first heard that phrase I thought it was something that only celebrities and very successful people need worry about. Their fans?

But we all have an eco-tribe around us. People who are taking energy, giving energy. It's not just Facebook that has a 'Boost' button. Some people we know will instantly give us that extra 'boost' – smile creators, energy providers, feelgood gifters. Your tribe are the people who pull and push you along, they encourage your progress.

Your tribe will be a diverse crowd. People will support you in many different ways. You will have the Hell Yeahs. This gang is full of positive affirmation for what you are doing, they will champion you, cheer you, tell you 'just do it' all the way home. Which is just what you need. There will also be the Yeah Buts. Don't dismiss the gang of Yeah Buts. This gang is still on your side. They get it,

'Surround yourself with both Hell Yeahs and Yeah Buts; you need them both. But move away from the Yeah Whatevers.'

they are just a bit more cautious. They are more reflective, thoughtful, think about the risks. They are worth listening to as well. You need Hell Yeahs and Yeah Buts in your life. They are on your side, in your tribe, they will give you different perspectives and possibilities. The people you don't need are the Yeah Whatevers, they don't get it, they aren't tuned in. That's OK – it doesn't mean they don't care about you, they just aren't tuned into your goals. Don't waste energy worrying about the Yeah Whatevers' reactions to what you are doing. They might be in our life for all sorts of reasons – family, neighbours, school connections . . . they aren't part of this vibe.

When I started my first online business, Snuggle Truffle, I had a handful of loyal, consistent customers who bought, posted, shared photos, left comments. I knew three of them. The rest discovered the brand, clicked with it, and joined the tribe. Some people sent me messages of encouragement, some sent me feedback and things they thought would help. They were all on my side, being in my tribe.

You don't know where your tribe will come from. Friends and family are a good place to start with a new idea, but they also may be the people holding you back.

If your immediate family don't 'get it' and fail to support your ideas, you have a few options. If the moment feels right it's good to try to explain why it's important to you, what you are planning, maybe even get them involved – or ask for their opinions.

If the situation feels in conflict, then you might have to go to ground. Creating a new direction without talking to family about it might feel lonely, it might feel uncomfortable, but it's OK – lots of people out there have done it. They use online and offline networks, people in the same situation, and they do it anyway.

Your friends and family might never get it. But this isn't about them. It's about you. Are you going to live in their doubt, or thrive in your passion? You will find people who will understand and get behind you.

They are out there now. Waiting to hear your ideas.

Where to find your tribe

- They might be just family and friends to start with, but don't waste energy on stressing if they aren't supportive.
- Go to local meetings – and if there isn't a local meeting, why not start one?
- Search for online groups and networks who represent your area of interest.
- Attend workshops and events with speakers who share your passion; again, if none exist, think about starting one.
- Start a blog or podcast – if you are writing or speaking about something you'll attract people to you.

Creating a plan, creating your story and having a tribe around you matter whether you are sticking, twisting or busting. Now let's get more specific on how to put your plans and stories into action.

How to Bust, But First Stick

If you want to start something new but need to get a job quickly you must be clear in your mind what your immediate priority is and what your long-term goal is. Manage your energy to match your priorities. Once you've achieved priority 1 then review your list and re-focus your energy onto priority 2, and so on.

Your priority list to 'bust but stick first' might look like this:

1. Get a job simply to earn some money (will reduce money worries).
2. Get a job that allows flexible working (will mean you can spend time with family).
3. Get a job that could reduce to four days a week (create space to develop side project).
4. Create time to start to develop side project (schedule in to focus energy – every Thursday evening).
5. Join a network community who are working in/ on an area similar to your long-term goal.

Even if you need to stick for now to bring in money you can still work towards your goal. This is about being in control of decisions, knowing why you are choosing to do something and how it's contributing to your long-term plan.

How to Stick and Get Your Ideal Job

There are a few options when you are searching for your next job. The purpose of the job, what you want from it and why you are doing it will come into your decisions. Your priority list will be a big factor.

The needs-must job

You aren't bothered what you do or who you do it for. You are doing this because you need to. Remind yourself why you are doing it (to pay the bills, probably). This job does not define who you are. You are enabling your future. Your aim is to do your best, look for opportunities, keep your long-term goal burning.

The foot-in-the-door job

You don't mind what you are doing, you really want to work for this organization. Remind yourself why you want to work here when you aren't thriving in your role (a foot in the door). Connect with people who do jobs you'd really like to do. Develop yourself in the role you'd really like. Set the intention of getting your ideal role (don't just settle for getting into the business).

The rebound job

You want that job, that title, that salary, that location. You don't mind who you are working for, it's the job that counts. It's good to be clear on why the job is important to do – why you do what you do. Watch out for values in the organization that might clash with your own. (You can do the job but can you put up with the workplace culture?) Would you be more comfortable doing a similar job in a different organization? Protect your energy levels from cultural corporate politics that don't matter to you.

The dream-case-scenario job

You are working for your ideal organization, in your ideal job. To get here you have done your research. You have put in the work to know who you are, what you are good at, you have been developing and working on yourself to get here. Great, but be aware of what you might be compromising outside work. Watch the hours you are putting in, watch the sacrifices, watch your health. You are thriving at work – but at what cost?

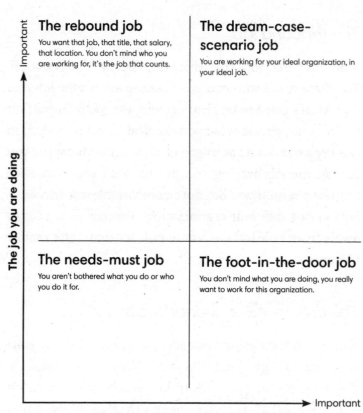

	The rebound job You want that job, that title, that salary, that location. You don't mind who you are working for, it's the job that counts.	**The dream-case-scenario job** You are working for your ideal organization, in your ideal job.

The needs-must job
You aren't bothered what you do or who you do it for.

The foot-in-the-door job
You don't mind what you are doing, you really want to work for this organization.

Important →

The organization you are working for

Do you know what your ideal job is?

If you feel like getting another job, what is your next step? Are you really clear about what the perfect role would look like? If your perfect scenario role came along tomorrow – what would it be? And why? Write down your answers to the following questions:

- Which businesses would you like to work for? Why? Is it because of their values? Their goals? Their status?
- Where is your perfect role located? Local? Within an hour's commute? Field based? Home based? Why is this important to you?
- What will you be doing in your role? Managing people? Delivering?
- How important is the organization you work for versus your role within it?

Depending on your immediate priorities there are a few options to consider when finding your next job. You might not necessarily be going for your 'dream job' scenario, it's the 'perfect next move to meet your needs right now' scenario that's more important.

How do you get your ideal job?

The first thing you must do is tell people what you're looking for. Tell everyone. Put it out there. Make clear what you want and why.

You won't get what you want unless people know what it is. This doesn't have to feel uncomfortable. If your goal has purpose, and reflects your why and your values, then it will come from a place of passion, enthusiasm and genuine drive.

- **Do your research.** If you've identified an industry, market or organization you want to focus on, find out who the major players are and who is in the role you'd like. Check their LinkedIn profiles; find out what they did to get there. Read up, form opinions, get involved with events and networks that are in this area.

- **Write about it and talk about it.** You don't have to be so direct as to post on LinkedIn: 'Wanted: job in market research'. You can do this, of course, and it does sometimes work, but you are likely to achieve better results, and a better job, by being creative and engaging. You can write articles on LinkedIn or use Medium – write about why you feel the market research industry is changing, what you observe, why you are still passionate about your industry. You can ask people for their opinions: 'I'm looking for my next opportunity in market research, what do you think are the most important skills for a researcher to have these days?'

- **Do not fear putting yourself out there.** Don't worry whether people will 'like', 'comment' or 'view' your posts and blogs. Many people will see and read articles but not engage. It's about putting out messages that signal what your intentions are – not about creating a fan club.

CV Dusting

When you lose your job, after first absorbing the news, the next thought is to go straight into solving this problem. Fight or flight. And how do you try to solve it? You dust off your CV. The CV, despite all progression of technology and ways of working, is still the number one document asked for when applying for a job, and therefore the first thing we think about when making a job change.

But it's just that, a document. It's a piece of paper. It's only ever as good as the reader's opinion. And you can't ever know what that is. So how do you get your CV into the best shape possible? The best thing you can do is make sure it reflects you, and what you are wanting to achieve.

There is a lot of advice out there about CVs. An overwhelming amount, in fact. But all you really need to do is use your CV to write yourself into your next move. If you are clear about what you want to happen next, write your CV to match that goal. Think of your CV as a magnet. If you put enough of what you want and who you are into it, and you are applying for a role that matches that, then the two will connect and attract.

Some tips and tricks

Before you dust off the old CV, get out your notebook and scribble down all the things you enjoyed about your past roles – what were your highest achievements, your favourite days, bits you looked forward to, bits you dreaded and all the things you miss now that you've left. Then use the following checklist to reshape your CV:

- Go through your scribbled list with a highlighter and pick out your best bits. Cross-reference with your CV. Does it feature all your highlights, best bits, and passions about your job?
- List on your CV all your previous jobs and use bullet points to break down the tasks you were responsible for and the key highlights/ achievements. Be as concise but as specific as possible. Add in stats and facts if you have them. It's important not to list only your job title and responsibilities; prospective employers want to know what you did and what you achieved.
- Don't include on your CV anything you don't want to do in your next role. If acquisitions and mergers was something you did, but you'd really rather not get involved ever again don't include it. Dial up the things that you do really want to do again, even if they comprised only a small part of what you did in your previous roles.
- Write in your own voice and include some personal information. That might take the form of a few details about yourself at the top or a

section on your passions outside work. This will help you to stand out from the crowd.

- Finally, if the application involves sending a CV and a covering letter, or filling in an online form, put your efforts into these areas. It matters. The people receiving them will be reading your words, and this is where you can really stand out. Be you and connect with the reader – speak to them.

In his book *The 7-Second CV* James Reed recommends:

1. *Keep it short and cut the fat. Only include what is relevant.*
2. *Capture the reader's attention. Demonstrate you are the perfect match.*
3. *If your experience doesn't marry up, work on demonstrating transferable skills.*
4. *Follow a logical, easy to navigate layout – don't be too fancy, make it easy to read, don't clutter the page.*
5. *Ditch clichés. Back up your attributes with examples of what you have delivered.*

James's book is a great place to start creating your CV. And as the title suggests, often you will only have seven seconds to grab the attention of the recruiter. Be intentional and care about your CV and application. Your effort will come through.

There is no one right way to do your CV. There are lots of experts and people who can help you create a CV that will work hard for you. But you always have to feel like it's yours, that you own it.

LinkedIn

First things first – are you on LinkedIn? You need to be. You'll enjoy it. It's where stuff happens!

Setting up your profile on LinkedIn

I asked Amanda Paradine, career coach and LinkedIn expert, how best to get started on LinkedIn. She gave me the following list:

1. Profile
Your Photo, Headline and Summary are the first things that people see when they visit your LinkedIn profile. These are giving visitors a snapshot of who you are and what you do – a bit like the trailer for a movie, these should draw a visitor in to make them want to watch the full film and read your full profile! Think about what you want your trailer to tell people.

2. Photo
Your photo needs to be up to date and professional-looking. Smiling is good!

3. Headline
Make it attention grabbing and include what you do and the value you provide. Incorporate keywords that

recruiters will be using to search: *Job Title, Location | Keyword | Keyword | Keyword.*

For example, *Human Resources Consultant, Suffolk | Recruitment | Training and Development | Employee Relations.*

4. Summary

Think about which keywords people will be using to find someone like you. For example, if you want to work as a project manager, include the term 'project manager' in your summary.

Avoid too many buzzwords like 'Hardworking' or 'Good attention to detail'. They are overused and take up valuable space on your profile which would be better if you include words that have more meaning and impact. Combine your aspirations and achievements in your summary. Write how you speak.

5. Skills

People that have more than five skills listed receive an average of seventeen times more profile views and are contacted much more often than those with fewer than five. Make a list of the skills you have that you can include and don't be shy about sharing your passions. You can include your technical and professional skills. LinkedIn recommend including skills like wine tasting and make-up artistry, even if they don't sync with your career skills.

The more you build up a comprehensive and unique profile, the better. I've seen 'cheese' as a skill in a LinkedIn profile, which just adds a touch of humanity and humour too; it would certainly make me more likely to contact that person.

6. Experience
The experience section gives you the chance to show what you've done and where you've done it and, importantly, gives you the chance to include exactly what you achieved.

7. Recommendations
Give and then receive! Provide recommendations and endorsements of skills for others and you'll find that others will then begin to do the same for you.

8. Stay active and up to date
To appeal to recruiters, keep your profile active and up to date. Post relevant industry articles to your homepage feed, 'like' articles others have posted and maybe even write and publish your own articles.

9. Add contacts
Search for companies you'd like to work for, connect with their recruiters, connect with people in the division you'd like to work in, connect with people in the industries you

want to move into. LinkedIn is a networking tool – use it
to uncover the 80 per cent of jobs that aren't advertised –
people will often post about jobs in their organizations
and recruiters use LinkedIn to advertise their roles as a
cost-effective way for them to get candidates.

The LinkedIn dilemma

Should you update your headline to say 'now available,
looking for a new opportunity, unemployed'? I think yes.
Well, maybe not the last one, but a version of the first two.
After all, you are these things. You are looking for new
opportunities. A lot of people lose their jobs; it's nothing to
be ashamed of. The quickest way to find opportunities
and get things moving is to tell people and open up.

If you are clear about what you want to do, include
that in your headline. If you want to find project freelance work, you can make your headline 'I help you get
your projects done'. If you want to attract a brand manager
role: 'Brand consultant – available now'. Be comfortable
with your headline and make sure it's working for you
even when you aren't there. LinkedIn will be your
hangout for the next few months so go transparent, put
yourself out there and tell people what you are looking
for and how you are going to help them. If you are feeling brave, get on camera, film yourself talking about
your situation and open yourself to people helping you

find your next role. Post about your experience, your opinions; ask questions. Demonstrate who you are and what you have to offer. Search for people in roles that are your ideal next move, or people who are doing similar things to what you want to start doing. Follow them, comment on their posts, and if you feel like you've got a connection send them a message. There are many different ways you can used LinkedIn to help you. My advice is to be truthful, transparent and helpful. It will go a long way for you. Once you have an 80 per cent feeling for what you are looking for, go for it.

Job Stalking

You applied for a job. You didn't even get an interview, or a 'thanks but no thanks'. Then on good old LinkedIn you see a post 'Congratulate Derek for starting a new position as VP for Product Development'.

Whhhhaaatttttt . . . that was the job I wanted. It was my dream job. I was perfect for it. Derek was hated by everyone in my office. I am much cleverer than Derek. Derek was so bad at his job he didn't even have a job. Why did Derek get it? Must be a mistake. I should write to them. Tell them they've made a dreadful mistake. Derek probably knows the CEO. Plays golf with him or something. I've got to call Paul about this. Wait until I tell him. He hated Derek. He won't believe it. Oh my God. Even Derek has a job. Derek can get a job. I can't get a job. There is no hope. Let's have some coffee, and Hobnobs.

Or.

Don't have the Hobnobs. Go for a walk. Derek is probably a nice guy. He has got bills too. Just move on. Don't waste your energy on other people. Keep focused on what you can do today to help yourself. If you are having a really bad day the best thing you can do is reach out to offer help to someone else. Wallow time is over. We are in Get Things Done mode now.

Applying for Jobs

You might feel like you need to get yourself out there as quickly as possible but CV spreading is not going to get you anywhere. It might get you a next move, but you might also find yourself in rebound territory. Be selective. Get out your priority list. Stick to your non-negotiables. Don't compromise. Only apply for jobs that you really want and you'll enjoy the process of applying for them.

Here are a few things you could try, to reduce the pain:

- Give yourself a quota. You can only apply for one job a day maximum.
- Get a cover letter template that you tweak each time.
- Try to apply via email rather than using online forms.

The rollercoaster that is the recruitment process

Once you've sent your CV and submitted your application, you sit back and wait – possibly for ever! Or you might get an email straight back asking you to come in for an interview the following day. The recruitment process is a rollercoaster, so try not to get too attached to the outcomes of applications and interviews. Once you've done the hard work applying, you have no control over the outcome. Use your energy on something else, or rest. Your next opportunity is getting closer, maintain your energy levels.

Should You Take the First Job You're Offered?

In a recent study by Another Door, 55 per cent of people who found jobs within three months of being made redundant ended up leaving them. It's common that the first job people take after being made redundant doesn't work out. Many don't feel happy after the first year of their next role and have started to look for a new role or change in career.

CASE STUDY – Jo

'I just felt trapped, again. I felt like I hadn't moved on since being made redundant sixteen months previously. In fact, things felt worse. I'd taken a pay cut and the job wasn't quite as challenging as I'd hoped. But I had a moment. I was out for a walk one weekend and thought "this can't go on". I started to fear that this was my life. I signed up to a social-media course, studied in the evenings, and within three months handed in my notice and set up as a social-media manager supporting local businesses. It was definitely the fear of staying in that cycle that scared me more than fear of leaving a safe job.'

The fear of being without work forces many people to rush straight back into employment, but often not on the right terms and for the wrong reasons. When deciding whether to take your first job offer, ask yourself why you are taking the job. Use your priority list and your values to check if it's the right move. Is the job aligned to your priorities right now?

How to Twist

If you want to stick to your field of expertise but change the way you do it your focus will be more on marketing, networking and repositioning yourself.

Twisting involves you reimagining the possibilities available to you. Your growth mindset is key to twisting. Being open to opportunity and stepping outside your comfort zone will help you reshape they way you use your skills and earn a wage.

How to become a freelancer

If you want to do the same thing you do now but in the capacity of freelancing or contracting then your focus will be on marketing yourself and letting people know what you do and how they can contact you.

You don't need to create a website to be a successful freelancer or contractor. Use your LinkedIn profile. You can set up a Medium blog if you want to share thoughts and articles.

Think about where your target organizations and clients hang out. Do they use Instagram or Facebook? Are they on Twitter? At the start focus on only one or two social-media platforms.

Whichever social media you use, make sure you are

absolutely crystal clear on what you do and who you help. Make yourself as findable as possible.

You don't even have to be on social media; you can just use your established network. Let people know what you are doing, contact ex-colleagues and previous employers.

Matthew Knight, founder of Leapers, an organization that supports the freelance community, outlines five things you need to consider before you take the leap of working for yourself:

1. **Active design.** *Figure out how you need to work.*
2. **Financial planning.** *Figure out what your money needs are, income and beyond.*
3. **Working relationships.** *Figure out how to work well with others.*
4. **Professional development.** *Figure out how you'll grow professionally.*
5. **Mental health.** *Figure out how to take care of yourself.*

Matthew says:

There's no one-size-fits-all solution to work. Everyone needs to find their own route to doing brilliant, meaningful, rewarding work – but this takes active design and consideration.

Don't take a leap without thinking about how you want to work, don't forget the things which create a foundation for doing brilliant work, and don't forget that just because you work for yourself, it doesn't mean you're by yourself.

Leapers is a great resource and support to get started as a freelancer.

How to start teaching others

You might want to twist and start passing on your skills and knowledge to others. You might want to become a teacher, a lecturer, a coach. You might want to start a business sharing your skills through workshops, online courses or events. Or share through writing a blog, writing a book or starting a podcast.

Here are five things to work through to get yourself up and twisting:

1. What new skills do you need? Do you need a training certificate, do you need to learn how to facilitate or teach?
2. Who are the people you want to teach or train? What are they doing now? Why will they choose you?
3. How will you deliver your service? Online courses? Face-to-face events? Through other institutions?

4. How will you market yourself? What are you comfortable doing? What help do you need to get yourself promoted and out there?
5. How do your competitors do it? What are the opportunities?

How to write a book

Is now the time to put down all your expertise into a book and twist yourself into an author?

You can start your writing career with a blog or by creating articles on Medium. You don't have to have an overwhelming need to create a blockbuster. Start by sharing your thoughts and ideas in short-form writing. You'll get a feel for the things you are enjoying writing about, and the things that resonate with people.

My agent, Jessica Killingley, also runs a writing academy where she helps entrepreneurs write and self-publish non-fiction. She shares the three most important things to consider to get you started on your book:

1. *Your book isn't about you, it's about your reader. So ask yourself what problem is your book solving for them.*
2. *If you are writing about experiences that you have been through personally, it's the thoughts, feelings and actions you took that make your book relatable and*

*valuable for your reader more than the specific
circumstances. What can your reader learn from your
mistakes or your resilience that they can apply to their
own situation?*

3. *Begin with the end in mind . . . What do you want to
happen with your book after it has been published?
What do you want to be known for? How can you
carry on helping your reader after they have finished
the book?*

Your book doesn't have to be the beginning of a huge
entrepreneurial endeavour, but think about who your
book is serving and how you build that community
around you while you are writing. Having an audience
ready and waiting to read it will help you get traction,
reach more people and make a bigger impact.

How to create a portfolio career

You don't have to decide one new path right now. You
can explore a few opportunities. You may be thinking
that you have a few ideas, many skills, a number of qualities that could be of service to people. You don't have to
be one thing. Do what you feel is right, have a good plan
to help people understand what you can do for them,
then get out there and talk about it! In a world where you
are told to have a niche, a portfolio career can feel like

you are going against the stream. And I get it. You have to build your personal brand, so people know what you are offering and how to work with you. But that brand can comprise a number of pillars. The key is to be aware of managing your energy, focusing your effort to match what you are offering to your target audience. You need to make it easy; people haven't got time to find out from you – you have to go to them. So yes, niching, like all good brand strategies, is a good idea. But it isn't the only way. You have a core focus, a core thing you are known for, but you can also have other interests, talents and things to offer.

In Emma Gannon's book *The Multi-Hyphen Method*, she says:

Multi-hyphenate careers are more common than you'd think. Look at celebrities if you want evidence. How many actors, singers, presenters now have clothing lines, podcasts, books . . . we find it completely acceptable. While it gets harder to answer the dinner party question, 'What do you do?' very succinctly, the excitement of a varied career is becoming increasingly attractive. The new multi-hyphenate career goes hand in hand with a need for more flexible working options. New research from online jobs site Timewise reveals that 60% of UK workers want access to a range of flexible working options.

The point of creating a portfolio career is to create a work life that fits around you. Portfolio careers might appeal to those who have many ideas, many skills and can adapt something they do very well to their circumstances.

Don't rule out developing a side project or several income streams. But do rule in the time it takes to get things going, and the amount of time, energy and resources you have to expend on each item in the portfolio.

This is where your 'why' and your priority list start to work hard for you. Balance is the key to success. If all your income streams are purely built on passion this might wear you out. If all your income streams are simply opportunities to make money, you might get rich but will you be satisfied, happy and fulfilled?

If all your income is earned from your expertise, are you confusing your customers who aren't quite sure what you do now? Having a range of ideas, a portfolio of services, can be rewarding, keep you fulfilled and put variety into your life. But that will work only if you like the idea of variety, juggling many different balls, multitasking and wearing lots of hats (feel free to insert your own clichés related to doing lots of things simultaneously). Work on how you can become known for one area first, then build on the others as side projects.

How to Bust

So, you are going bold! You are going for it. It's time to leap and bust it out, throw it all in the air and start something completely new. Whether it's a new business, or retraining, or going travelling, busting out should feel liberating, energized, right. Yes, it might take hard work, and lots of relearning, and new learning, but your purpose will drive you onwards.

Starting a business

Your time of self-reflection might have brought you to the conclusion that you'd like to choose bust and throw in your old career for something new and start your own business. This is an exciting, but daunting time.

How do you know if you've got a great idea for a business?

When you've got an idea for a business give yourself scheduled time to play with the concept in a structured way that will help focus your energy and thoughts.

The idea wheel is a simple process you can work through to test your business idea.

'By finding and following what excites you, you'll help to give your life real meaning and your business its mojo. The path to a profitable business starts with recognizing where your passion lies. And don't just think "What do I enjoy?" but rather "Which problems do I see that need addressing that get me excited?"'

Laurence McCahill, Happy Startup School co-founder

The idea wheel

1. **The customer's problem**
   - Every business is solving a problem for the customer. Customers are always buying solutions.
   - What is the problem your idea is solving for the customer?
   - Why is this a problem?
   - How is the problem being solved right now?
   - Are there leaders/role models to follow?

2. **Know your customer**
   - Who is your audience? Give them a name, describe their lifestyle.
   - What is the role your idea plays in their life?
   - Who is your buyer? (This might be someone other than the consumer.)

3. **The need**
   - Why do your audience need your idea right now?
   - What will be missing in their lives without it?
   - What will change in their lives with it?

4. **Your USP**
   - What is your unique selling point? Why will they buy from you/your business?

- Why can you deliver the idea better than someone else?
- Why are you the expert (the authority)?

5. **The competition**
   - How is the problem being solved today?
   - What would people buy instead of your idea?
   - Who is already doing this (or similar)? How can you be better than them?

6. **Your needs**
   - What skills and knowledge do you need?
   - What support do you need?
   - What resources do you need?

7. **How will you sell this?**
   - How will people know about you?
   - What is your storyline?
   - How will people buy from you?

You know what your idea is. You know why you want to do it. Working around the idea wheel will help you to understand the size of the how. The idea wheel should work to help you feel that it is possible for your idea to become reality.

The Idea Wheel

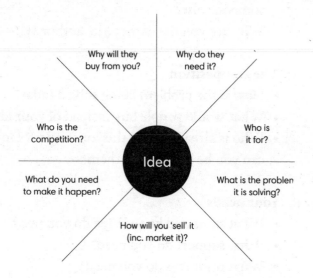

Why will they
buy from you?

Why do they
need it?

Who is the
competition?

Who is
it for?

Idea

What do you need
to make it happen?

What is the problem
it is solving?

How will you 'sell' it
(inc. market it)?

A simple start

You don't have to have everything all lined up and ready to go before you launch.

Things you don't need to do to start:

- You don't need to spend time on the name of your company/brand before you know what it does/what it stands for/what it will serve.
- You don't need to spend time (and money) on a logo before knowing why this matters to

you and why it matters to your (potential) customers.

- You don't need to spend time creating a website (because you've ignored the two points above and already have a name and logo) before you know what your customers want.

'Nobody is ever ready to begin. We want a few practice rounds . . . Bad news: You'll never be ready. You'll never be fully prepared and the conditions will never be perfect . . . You just have to start . . . Ready. Fire. Aim.'

James Victore, Feck Perfuction

Brand Before Logo

Lucy Griffin-Stiff runs a programme called Brand Before Logo. Lucy works with people starting out and focuses them on the what and why before they get to do the creative stuff. Lucy will hold someone in the what and why position longer than Heathrow control tower, until they are ready to approach the runway and land the how. Lucy says:

> 'I see entrepreneurs diving straight into the details of how they will do something and wasting time on the look and feel of their business, website, collateral without spending time thinking about what it is that customers want from them. You can have the best-looking website in the world but if it doesn't have the right offer or connection it's pointless.'

For those of us who like the HOW, it's a bit like when you move into a new house and you just want to put pictures on the wall and spend time thinking about where to put your Emma Shipley cushion, rather than cleaning the skirting boards, painting the walls, scrubbing the carpet. But to create the right foundations for your business and spend money on the right things to maximize impact and efficiencies, then focus we must on WHATs and WHYs.

Five things you can do now to start your business for free

1. Create a Facebook business page (and/or Facebook group) – see great examples of people who have started a Facebook group and evolved it into a business: Helen Hamston, founder of Mummy's Gin Fund; Jen Gale, founder of Sustainable(ish); Jane Johnson, founder of Careering into Motherhood; Katy Fridman, founder of Flexible People.

2. Start a blog – you don't have to create a website blog to start blogging. You can create a page on Medium, or use articles on LinkedIn. If you have something to say it's about getting your message out there.

3. Create a business identity – if you need a business identity or a logo to help you get started there are ways to do it without spending a lot of money. (Remember you don't need it, but you might want it to help you feel like it's real.) Tailorbrands.com create free logos. Canva.com has a free service where you can create a simple identity. Or just choose three colours and a font and start to use them consistently in all you do from now on. You can create a more defined brand, and work with

an expert, when the time is right and the investment is worthwhile.

4. Volunteer your services – you can approach your local charity, school, hospital or council and offer the services that you are developing. Think of organizations or communities who would benefit from your offer and pitch to them.

5. Offer to speak at events – if you believe in your idea you'll be sufficiently passionate about it to be able to speak about it. Find local events where you can start talking to people about what you are doing. It's a great way to acquire testimonials as well as hear yourself living what you want to achieve.

Moments of Urgh!

Becoming unstuck is about planning, building confidence and putting yourself out there. It's an exciting time, and hugely energizing as possibilities and ideas get closer to becoming realities.

There will also be moments of urgh! So to handle these moments we build them into our unstuck plans. We know they are going to happen, so let's just identify what they are and what to do with them.

Butterflies

That strange fluttery feeling when you are waiting to hear about an interview, a job, a client. I found it fascinating that even jobs that I definitely didn't want still evoked this sensation! I guess it's the same as being dumped, that dreaded 'it's not you, it's me'. The fear of rejection. Even when you know it wasn't the right job, or a job you wanted. It's the fact they didn't want you either.

Is there any way to deal with this feeling? Gin? Sex? Chocolate? Distraction?

It was the final straw for me when I found myself, yet again the week before Christmas, getting butterflies, feeling sickly in my stomach, nervous tingles in my fingertips, when the recruitment agency number flashed up on my phone. And they can never just leave a message that says, 'Well done, you've got it' or 'Sorry, you haven't'. It has to be a drawn-out drama – 'I have feedback to share with you' – like they are Simon Cowell on *Britain's Got Talent*.

And the feedback, once you do get back in touch with them: 'Oh, the other person just was more "strategic" and had a bit more experience.' Wouldn't you just love to know the real reason one day? Real, actual reasons, such as (made up but possible):

1. Your face was too round.
2. They were intimidated by your clear, higher calling and wisdom.
3. They did not like your shoes.
4. You were two minutes late. (Turns out it did matter.)
5. You didn't laugh at their joke.
6. You were too tall.
7. You were a bit boring.
8. You were a bit weird.
9. You were at the wrong interview. (No one liked to say.)
10. There was no job.

Or

11. Derek got the job. He always was going to get the job. You never had a chance. You were just part of the game they play.

Sometimes you and the job just aren't a good fit. Remember, even if you've done the work on your story, magic can only happen when things align. There will be many reasons you don't get a job, don't win a pitch, have quiet business times. Anticipating and overthinking the whys and what ifs won't help you. Butterflies are just there to help your nervous system cope. If you are getting anxious, distract yourself. Take a walk, watch a film, go swimming, read. Do something to lose yourself in for a while. The outcome is not going to be changed by the level of your anxiety.

Rejection

'We have taken the time to review your application, and unfortunately at this stage we have decided not to take the process further. We feel that we have sufficient candidates who better suit the requirements of the role. We sincerely hope that you continue to follow our brand, and we wish you the best of luck in your search for a new position.' Why? Why would I follow your brand and be reminded of how you find other people more suitable?

Well – you can stick it. And I'm taking my money elsewhere. You've not just lost a great employee, you've lost a customer. I mean, you could say this is a bit extreme. But it's true. I have boycotted several brands because of their 'sorry you didn't get the job' emails (not because I didn't get the job). It's very satisfying for a while. And then it gets tricky. And possibly a bit pointless.

You didn't get the job.

You didn't get the contract.

You didn't win the business.

Repeat.

Repeat.

Repeat.

When you've already been made redundant, rejection can feel like it is becoming a bit of a theme.

You feel rejected from your now redundant job.

You feel rejected you didn't get the job.

It's upsetting.

You can be upset.

Then pick yourself up again and go again.

So embrace rejection as part of the process.

If you want to feel differently about rejection, watch Jia Jiang's TED talk 'My 100 Days of Rejection'. You will never feel bad about being rejected again.

Don't Ask for Feedback

It's tempting to ask for feedback and get people's opinions to help you progress. Some feedback is useful, some feedback is not so useful. Feedback is not always a gift. It's someone's opinion. That's all it is. Feedback is the noise when the speakers squeal. It hurts your ears. If you want advice from people you admire or value, then that's a whole different ball game. So rather than 'I'm not getting any results from my CV, any feedback?', reframe the question – 'I'm aiming for roles as a sales manager, do you have any advice on how you'd position yourself?'

You'll feel better about asking. You'll get better quality advice and shared experience that you can then analyse and decide whether it will work for you. When people ask for feedback they end up with a list of things they feel they must improve. That's the wrong way of looking at it. It's just a list of opinions. Opinions that might say more about them than about you. When people share their views it often has everything to do with how they would feel or react and nothing to do with your position. You need to view 'feedback' opinions through your own lens of what you want to get out of something. The best feedback is not feedback, it is advice.

Watching what others do, and following role models,

then lining it up against your behaviours and actions can be far more powerful. Feedback can start to set you back, not propel you forward, so think carefully about how to get connection and advice from people.

'You can listen to what people say, sure. But you will be far more effective if you listen to what people do.'

Seth Godin

Comparing

There is a fine line between looking towards role models for inspiration and unhelpfully comparing yourself to others. Sometimes it's easy to get drawn into feeling that everyone else has got life sorted and they're happier, more confident, successful and fulfilled than you. That is what social media says anyway. But it's important that you accept that everyone is on a different path. Comparing yourself to others whom you perceive to be better or brighter than you will only hold you back. Tune into you and focus on your goals. Reframe and look at other people's success as a signal that it's possible and that you should keep going. If they can do it, so can you.

Tiny Habits Create Big Change

You have been making some big decisions about your career and your life. Huge goals are exciting, but to achieve them you'll need to break them down into tiny steps. These will build the foundations to make sure your long-term life goals are achieved. In his book *Tiny Habits*, Dr B. J. Fogg talks about this approach, explaining that only three things will change behaviour in the long term:

- **Option A** – Have an epiphany.
- **Option B** – Change your environment.
- **Option C** – Take tiny steps.

Fogg states, 'You have to create new habits through small steps, not by addressing old bad habits. Old bad habits can be worked on but only by replacing them with new ones.'

Your work on your priority list will help you be clear on what change you really want and the importance it has to you. Why something is important matters. It's your reason to make changes, to take small steps. Tiny habits only work if you want the changes to happen. *Want*. How much do you want it? To make losing your job the best thing that ever happens to you, you will need to make changes. Making changes to get the results you want

'When you are trying to make changes in your life it may feel overwhelming. Start with tiny, so tiny it's laughable.'

'You can achieve amazing things, but you have to be single minded, and single focused. You have to want the change.'

Mike Coulter, Tiny Habits coach

doesn't have to feel hard, but it does need to be intentional. Go back and review your list. Does it contain the changes you want, or the changes someone else wants?

Tiny habits will help you achieve change in all areas of your life. Mike Coulter explains in his workshop called Tiny Habits, 'Changing the way you live and behave won't happen overnight (if ever), you need to break things down to tiny enough things you'll easily achieve, so tiny they are laughable.' Mike shares his story of how he created time to meditate by putting his chair outside every morning. That was all he did for a while, just put his chair outside. Then one day he sat on it. And then one day he sat a bit longer. And now he meditates every day.

Putting a chair outside every day sounds odd, maybe even ridiculous. But what he is describing is no different from how people describe their route to addiction, a small indulgence that slowly became an everyday habit. When the mind plants the seed of an idea, it also suggests the route to growing into a full-on tree.

When you have planted a seed of your business idea there are now only two things it might do – grow or die. Are you going to nourish it, keep it watered, pay attention to it, or will you let it wither?

You want to do fifty push-ups a day? Start with one. You want to change what you do for a living? Start by telling yourself about it. You want to start a business? The first step is to plant the seed.

How to Create a Tiny Habit Recipe

Pick behaviours YOU want, not things you should do, or someone else wants you to do.

- Identify an existing habit and use it as a trigger (anchor the moment).
- Do the small habit straight after the trigger.

Build in 'feelgood' immediately after the behaviour (shout 'Awesome!' . . . Go on, us Brits are great at that kind of thing.)

Celebrate your wins

At the Tiny Habits workshop Mike made us all think about how we celebrate. (Probably not great that most of us said 'glass of wine'.) He made us think about it some more. He talked about the power of reward and how recognizing achievement, no matter how small, creates an impression in the mind that will trigger it to feel good next time it happens. In sport psychology, footballers, tennis players, athletes, swimmers are encouraged to celebrate as part of their training. Celebrating makes us want something more, gives us that 'let's do it again' feeling, but it can also make us fear failure more, as if we now have more to lose. Tiny habits help that fear

'Plant a good seed in the right place and it will grow without further coaxing.'

Dr B. J. Fogg

'Emotions create habits, the stronger you feel a positive emotion from the tiny habit, the more you'll do it again and add to it.'

Mike Coulter

of failure feel less of a risk, so we keep progressing forward.

Our negative bias, which keeps us safe and minimizes risk, can unfortunately also keep us stuck. To change something in your life you have to start somewhere. Tiny habits put you over the line towards change, all you have to do is keep looking forward and not take a step back. Take small achievable steps and you'll start to create the shift.

We have three types of habit:

1. Bad habits (they don't contribute to our goal, but we spend time doing them).
2. Neutral habits (we just do them because we have to).
3. Positive/contributing habits (we do them and they make positive contributions to moving forward).

The idea is to replace the bad habits with positive habits, by attaching tiny habits to things we already do (neutral habits). When you switch on the kettle in the morning, do something straight after it to start making a change . . . such as putting out your yoga mat.

Sharing your goal celebration and the change you want to make helps you. You don't always get support from obvious places like friends and family; sometimes outside help is the extra support you need. There is a

Facebook group for everything these days. There are network groups and social events to meet like-minded people. The Meet Up app is a great place to start looking for events local to you. The website Stick creates an online community to help you stick to goals.

The Struggle is Real

If you keep finding yourself thinking this all sounds lovely, but it's not really that simple, you are right. Well, kind of. It isn't straightforward. For some people, things just fall into place. But. For the majority of people life is a slog. It's like the motivational guru Gary Vaynerchuk says, 'Smart work will never replace hard work, it only supplements it . . . stop whining, start hustling.' So, things might not work out first go. It might feel like things aren't going to happen. Never lose sight of your priority list. Never rip up your 'why'. Never let go of your dream job.

Yes, it's sometimes going to feel like a massive struggle. It's sometimes going to feel uncomfortable. And sometimes you are going to want to give up. But give up and do what? Work on how you manage your struggle, not on how you fight your struggle. Join the Another Door community and share all your woes. That's what it's there for; work on yourself every day. You'll keep improving how you face the shit head-on until it barely becomes anything to you. Those 3 a.m. wake-up sweats will become ideas, not worries, and those tears of despair will become tears of joy. It just all might take a bit longer than you want. And you might meet a few detours, false turns and cul-de-sacs along the way.

If you have to go off track for a while, don't stop putting

things out there, blogging, talking, meeting people, telling them your goals. Don't stop any of it. If you've had to take a contract instead of developing your business, then the place you now work is your client (not your place of work). And it's actually a great contract you've just won.

If you've had to take a part-time job to keep enough funds coming in, then you've actually just secured funding for your business venture. If you've had to take a job that doesn't tick all your priority list boxes, then you've bought some time while you develop your thoughts and look for inspiration on what to do next. There is always a positive way to look at things. Just keep monitoring how much time you are spending worrying about things not working out versus how much time you are doing stuff to move things on. We've said it before, we both know – it doesn't matter that you will be doing things and they might not be an overnight sensation.

The struggle is real. Things won't just happen immediately. And if you've heard about Linda who has just landed her dream job, you know what to do. Delete. Delete. Delete. If you have to do something that doesn't quite tick all the boxes yet, reframe it to write into your plan. But onwards we must go.

Becoming Unstuck

Becoming unstuck is an incredibly liberating feeling. You've probably forgotten you've been made redundant at all. Now all your thoughts are about the future. It doesn't mean everything becomes easy. It does mean you are now in control.

Top tips to becoming unstuck

- Spend time on creating a simple plan of action.
- Spend time on creating your story.
- Spend time on creating a tribe who will keep you moving forward.

When you've decided what you want to do, whether it's to stick, twist or bust, the next move is to take small, planned steps forward, and remain open to opportunity without getting hung up on end goals and outcomes.

It's now all about solving issues that move you forward, not dwelling on things in the past. You've got your plan, you know your story, you are building your tribe, you know your choices. It's time to thrive.

Part 5

Thrive

Are You Ready to Thrive?

To say you are thriving when you are working through so much change in your life might feel awkward. Thriving is a personal thing. When you are thriving you are in the place you want to be, and need to be. Things might not be perfect, but you are in control. You know why you are doing what you are doing, you are making conscious decisions, your actions are based on a clear intention of the outcomes you want to achieve. As you work through this final part of the book, keep the following points in mind:

1. Thriving is something that inherently happens on your own terms. The key thing to think about at this stage is what does success look like for *you*? This should not be based on external factors but on your own individual measure of success.
2. It is about facing your fears, taking on self-doubt and working on self-belief.
3. It is about seeing failure, setbacks and rejection as part of progress.
4. It is about letting go of things holding you back and living in the realm of possibility.
5. It is when your priorities, your energy and your focus are all aligned.

Thriving does not mean that everything is perfect, or even that things are generally going your way. Instead, it indicates that you are working on yourself so that you can handle all that comes from setting yourself goals – setbacks, rejection, failures, wobble days, insecurities and those days when you want to quit. It means looking after yourself, celebrating little successes and surrounding yourself with people who encourage you onwards. Your evolution is endless, so will always have ups and downs, but thriving is about being open to opportunity and accepting that those ups and downs come with living in a space of progress and growth.

What Do You Really Want?

Hurrah! We have reached the final part of the book and, hopefully, you are feeling like you are about to start a new chapter. What happens next is up to you.

So what do you want? ('Really, really want', as the Spice Girls would say. No apologies for the Spice Girls reference, Victoria Beckham is the best example of following what you really really want despite the barriers you might think are in your way.)

Have you started taking action, putting yourself out there, telling people what your plans are? Have things already started to change?

If you have worked through your priority list and you really want to deliver it then you have a clear way forward.

Equally, having a clear view of what you do not want can be just as empowering. Try flipping your 'don't wants' to see what they do look like, for example 'I don't want to work in an office any more' flips into 'I want to work outdoors, in the fresh air with animals.'

Make sure your priority list has clear wants, in as much detail as possible. So much detail you can almost smell it, taste it, touch it.

You've Come a Long Way

You've invested time to read this book so, hopefully, you already have a sense that what has happened to you is an opportunity.

It is normal to have doubts and fears.

If you have had a long, established career, or a vocational job like medicine that you studied long and hard for, then it's natural to feel like it was all for nothing if you make changes now.

You may feel that if your existing knowledge and skills are not used in the same way then all of the past will have been a waste. Perhaps you are thinking that rather than changing you should just stick and plough on. If so, you are succumbing to the sunk-cost fallacy.

The sunk-cost fallacy is an idea coined by Hal Arkes and Catherine Blumer, which exposes a common fallacy that it is a mistake to abandon a project when we've invested many resources including time, money or effort in it. It isn't a mistake if you don't actually want to continue doing the same thing, if you aren't getting what you want out of it or if it is not serving any purpose for you. Your past should not control your future. Your future should control what you do now. Use your experience but do not let it hold you back.

Believe That You Can (and Have to) Make Changes

To thrive, and to make losing your job the best thing that happened to you, you must see it as a wake-up call. Maybe you have always wanted to change things, to do something different, but that dream has become lost in the day to day. This is your moment. You have permission to pursue what you really want to.

You Can Have an Impact

If you have an idea, a dream or a goal that you want to achieve then you must believe that you are going to have an impact on more people than just yourself alone.

Hang on. Don't run away. That's not as overwhelming as it sounds. You don't have to bring about world peace. However, your idea for change should involve others. The moment you realize that what you want to do is bigger than just you, it becomes your mission. There is no choice but to pursue it. Whether it's to get a job in your ideal organization and make a difference to what it is trying to achieve, whether it's teaching others what you know and passing on your experience, or starting a brand-new business to deliver something that people need. Whatever you decide, you are having an impact on people, so it matters to them as well as to you.

If you have a business idea – what problem are you solving?

If you want another job – how can you help the business/your manager improve?

When you start to better yourself, you are going to make life for people around you better too.

You are going to have an impact.

When times get bumpy it is good to remind yourself of the effect you have on the people around you. You make a difference, and it can be a positive one.

Be the better manager, the better leader, the better business owner, the better specialist.

What have you done today to make an impact?

At the end of every day, take ten minutes to think about every decision and action you made during the past twenty-four hours, and what the impact was on you and others.

Stuff on the list could be:

- Your decision to say no to the 5p plastic bag. The impact: one less plastic bag in circulation.
- Your decision to sort out your wardrobe and drop off a big bag to the charity shop. The impact: someone else can enjoy your much loved but not much worn clothes while a charity benefits from extra money.
- Your decision to go for a run. The impact: you can eat more for lunch. (Just kidding – of course it's about being healthy, which benefits those who care about you.)

All these things affect something or somebody today.

It does not have to be a big, life-changing difference; even the smallest things add up and will have an effect, a consequence.

'If you think you are too small to have an impact, try going to bed with a mosquito.'

Anita Roddick

In addition, what you do and the impact you have on others also forms your personal story, your personal brand – it's how people will make decisions about you and your business. It could be the difference that gets you that job or wins that order.

No one can be perfect, and we can all have our off days, but more conscious living may help us make a more useful contribution.

Create a Mindset to Thrive

Mindset. It can hold us back. It can propel us forward.

Psychologist Carol Dweck studied mindset and identified two types: fixed and growth.

The fixed mindset believes you can be good at something only if you are born with the talent. You say, 'It's just not me.' You don't believe there is much you can do to change the situation. You accept your lot.

Watch out for these thoughts creeping in . . .

- 'I'm really bad at that.'
- 'I forget everything all the time.'
- 'I never finish stuff.'
- 'I can't do that.'
- 'It's all right for them . . .'

You are talking yourself out of something. You are convincing yourself there is a very good reason not to do something. You are making excuses.

There might be things in your past that reinforce your belief. However, don't let your past hold back your future.

Someone with a growth mindset believes that anything is possible, that things are worth a try, that they can learn, that it's worth trying again and again.

And they have thoughts more like these:

- 'I'll have a go.'
- 'It's OK to make mistakes.'
- 'I'll keep trying.'
- 'Attempting new things is the only way to learn.'
- 'Other people's success inspires me to persevere, and shows me it's possible.'

If you really want something, you need your growth mindset to help you get there. You need to decide you want this enough to change and work on yourself to get the success you desire.

CASE STUDY – Virginia

'When I was made redundant, it was unexpected, sudden and scary but also exciting in an odd way too. I knew it was not personal as it affected everyone in the building. I enjoyed the break initially but soon got bored of the long days of job hunting.

'So I created a routine of exercise and job hunting in the mornings with time off in the afternoon. I made the most of the outplacement provided by my former company, which was fantastic personal development for me. The coaching was particularly helpful and I followed all the advice and leads with great gusto. I also had coffee with as many people and recruiters as possible as I learned the value of networking.

'Over a period of a few months, I wrote letters [this was 1999] to all the heads of communication in the FTSE100 pitching for work. I always wrote that I would call the following week. It was not easy to make those calls every Friday but I did get several interviews, which inspired me to keep going. The one that delivered was to my old boss, who was moving to a new firm and had, surprisingly to me, been expecting my call. Just a few days later, I had a job offer.

'Although this was twenty years ago, the lessons of persistence, taking advice, sharing stories and ideas with fellow job-hunters, following up every single lead are still just as relevant today.

'I have often wondered about luck and I think it is about being positive and channelling energy into what you do. My way out of redundancy was all about timing but, as people say, you create your own luck. So that would be my advice. Believe in luck, be positive and always energetic (and if you are not in the right place for it on any given day, take the day off).'

'Hello Fear, Nice to Meet You'

Fear can come along when it's least expected and, if you're not ready for it, throw you off course. Grabbing hold of the fear and taking it on will not just move it out of the way, it will give you extra energy to keep going. It's a bit like the 'revenge' energy we talked about in Part 1. Fear can power you forward.

If you just don't think you can do it or you don't trust yourself, here are five things to help you power through from Susan Jeffers's book *Feel the Fear and Do It Anyway*.

- *FEAR TRUTH #1 The fear will never go away as long as you continue to grow! Every time you take a step into the unknown, you experience fear. There is no point in saying, 'When I am no longer afraid, then I will do it.' You'll be waiting for a long time. The fear is part of the package.*
- *FEAR TRUTH #2 The only way to get rid of the fear of doing something is to go out and . . . do it! When you do it often enough, you will no longer be afraid in that particular situation. You will have faced the unknown and you will have handled it. Then new challenges await you, which certainly add to the excitement in living.*
- *FEAR TRUTH #3 The only way to feel better about yourself is to go out and . . . do it! With each little*

step you take into unknown territory, a pattern of
strength develops. You begin feeling stronger and
stronger and stronger.

- *FEAR TRUTH #4 Not only are you afraid when
facing the unknown, so is everyone else! This should
be a relief. You are not the only one out there feeling
fear. Everyone feels fear when taking a step into the
unknown. Yes, all those people who have succeeded in
doing what they have wanted to do in life have felt the
fear – and did it anyway. So can you!*
- *FEAR TRUTH #5 Pushing through fear is less
frightening than living with the bigger underlying fear
that comes from a feeling of helplessness!*

This is the one truth that some people have difficulty
understanding. When you push through the fear, you
will feel a sense of relief as your feeling of helplessness
subsides. You will wonder why you did not take action
sooner. You will become more and more aware that you
can truly handle anything that life throws at you. Being
fearless is not about being reckless. If you fear something,
you have to address it. There may be good reasons why
you have fear. Do not avoid fear. Listen to it. Embrace it.
Feel it. It will help you to keep going.

Taking on the Ghosts

Once you have started on your mission to get a new job or start something new the only thing stopping you thriving will be you. You are now in a head-on battle – with yourself.

Just like Pac-Man, you need to keep focused on getting the cherries and keep away from those ghosts!

They will be hunting you down.

Did you know the original ghosts of Pac-Man all had different names and personalities?

- Inky (the blue one), or Bashful, is the fickle one, very unpredictable, had no way of really knowing the next move. Inky was meant to be the smartest ghost, but he lacked focus and so rarely caught Pac-Man.
- Blinky (the red one), or Shadow, is the chaser, known to follow Pac-Man really closely, resulting in Pac-Man panicking and making hasty decisions.
- Pinky (the pink one), or Speedy, is always trying to be ahead of Pac-Man and spoil Pac-Man's plans.
- Clyde (the orange one), or Pokey, is known for 'feigned ignorance', getting close to Pac-Man

but then retracting at the last minute, then having a burst of energy in another direction before stopping again.

Inky, Blinky, Pinky and Clyde were the original ghosts. They were created with 'hustling' personalities, designed to do everything in their power to distract, pressurize and hustle Pac-Man into making errors. If Pac-Man was caught then that was his fault alone.

You are going to have a few ghosts running around after you, trying to keep you away from the cherries.

(Are we really going to use Pac-Man ghosts to talk about mindset? It looks like we are . . .)

- Inky – No focus, likes to procrastinate, finds excuses.
- Blinky – Puts on the pressure, never lets it be, causes worry and unsettling feelings.
- Pinky – Likes to be ahead all the time, thinking of all the reasons why things won't be, so gets overwhelmed with the enormity, worries about comparison.
- Clyde – Burst of energy helps but hinders when momentum is lost. Clyde suffers from not feeling good enough. Sometimes he gets over it but then it hits him again.

How many ghosts are chasing you? If you are going to reach your goal, and eat those cherries, you need to recognize them and work hard to get away. Just like the Pac-Man game became easier the more you practised, so when these ghosts are hunting you down you need to work hard to move away and evade them.

Finding a Superhero to Come to Your Rescue

Actually, there are no superheroes.

Sorry.

It seems like there are quick answers sometimes, especially when you look online. Headlines offering quick solutions like 'This is why you aren't moving on', etc. are generally just marketing by someone trying to sell you something. There is nothing inherently wrong with that but don't think that there is anyone out there who can swoop into your life and sort it all out. Only you can do that.

Once you have identified where you want to be then the next step is figuring out what help you need to get there. (And once you have that it may well feel like a superhero actually has come along to rescue you.)

To know what the right help is for you, we have to go back to being stuck.

WAYS OF BEING STUCK

Stuck in the idea – I have an idea, but cannot take the leap.

Stuck in the 'why' – I don't know why I'm doing this, I don't have purpose.

Stuck in the 'what' – I don't know what I'm doing.

Stuck in the 'how' – I don't know how to do it.

Stuck in the 'who' – I don't know who I am.

Now you can use that stuckness to figure out where you need help:

- Where are you stuck?
- What's stopping you from moving forward?
- What is the most immediate help you need right now?
- What can you do yourself?
- Where do you need help?

The most important thing here is to clarify what help you want right now and stay focused on that.

So find that superhero solution within yourself. (But don't find Spiderman if you aren't looking to crawl up walls today.)

Potholes and Ditches

At this point, you might be in flow, but there may still be something holding you back.

Perhaps your confidence is low. Or you feel disheartened by your progress. Your brain is trying to protect you from making a bad decision but in doing so it's preventing real change.

- 'You can't do that, you don't have the skills.'
- 'You can't do that, no one will believe you.'
- 'You can't do that, no one will listen.'
- 'You can't do that, you aren't good enough.'

When my daughter started riding a bike for the first time she set off with gusto and determination. Then she hit a pothole and fell off. 'I can't do it, Mummy,' she said. For her there had only been one possible outcome, succeed or fail. In her view, she had failed.

After a bit of debate she got back on and tried again. And tried again. And again. And again. Things were getting muddy. We started to sing a song. 'I can, I can, I will,' we sang (shouted, really . . . Not much of a song, I know, but even Lennon and McCartney had to start somewhere.) Off she went hurtling down the road shouting, 'I can, I can, I will,' as she forgot to turn and ended up in the ditch. Yes, you will, my love, you will indeed.

Don't waste time arguing with yourself about if you are good enough, whether you can do it, if anyone will care. The best way to find out is do a few things. Throw some stuff out there and see what happens.

You can't quit something you haven't started. You can't give up until you've tried.

When you feel like quitting before you've even begun, go back to the start. That doesn't mean starting again from scratch. It means reminding yourself why you want to do this.

You have decided you want to do something. You know why. So remember that. And get help if you need it.

Being an Imposter

A little warning as you begin to get successes and wins. You might start to think, 'Is this really happening?' Imposter syndrome is the feeling you are deceiving others. It's a little voice inside saying, 'This won't last, you've got lucky so far, you are winging it, they'll find out, you don't deserve this.'

It stops you celebrating your achievements. It gets in the way of progress. It holds you back from accepting opportunities.

The term 'imposter syndrome' was first introduced in a 1978 article about female high achievers, and their feeling, despite their success, that they didn't deserve it. The article was 'The Impostor Phenomenon in High Achieving Women: Dynamics and Therapeutic Intervention', by Pauline Clance and Suzanne Imes. Since then, imposter syndrome has been used in wider coaching and support practices to help women and men, young and old, to overcome their doubts. Dr Valerie Young, an expert on the subject, has categorized it into five subgroups:

The Perfectionist – *The inability to let things go until they are perfect. This can lead to not trying out new things for fear it won't be good enough. Perfectionism can galvanize you to producing great work, but it can also paralyse you into not producing any.*

Perfection is in the eye of the beholder. What you believe to be perfect, another person may not value. The quest for perfection is wasted energy. It's OK to set yourself standards, but if your standards are holding you back then what is the point of them? Nothing happening because it's not perfect is always worse than something happening which can still be worked on.

__The Superhuman__ – Sending that one last email before you go home, jumping back on email when you get home, taking on extra jobs that you don't have time for and working on weekends rather than relaxing and enjoying yourself. You think downtime is a waste of time. Impostor workaholics are addicted to the validation that comes from working, not to the work itself.

It's dangerous because you can start resenting your job, resenting the project you are working on, resenting people, instead of enjoying moments for what they are. Is your time away from work now a chance to reset. What came up in your life dashboard (page 76) that might help you relate to this?

__The Natural Genius__ – They judge their competence based on ease and speed rather than effort. If they take a long time to master something, they feel shame. The success bar is set impossibly high. Natural geniuses do not

*just judge themselves based on ridiculous expectations,
they also judge themselves based on getting things right
at the first try. When they are not able to do something
quickly or fluently, their alarm sounds.*

More commonly known as the smartass, clever clogs
or know-it-all. Unable to comprehend that others might
be able to help. Believe a setback is a failure. If you don't
think you'll win, you won't even start. If it's not in your
comfort zone, you wouldn't consider it. Watch out that
your natural genius isn't stopping you from trying new
things.

*The Soloist – People who feel as though asking for help
reveals their phoniness. It's OK to be independent, but
not to the extent that you refuse assistance so that you
can prove your worth.*

Asking for help can be hard. It can feel like you are
admitting defeat. Most success stories involve asking for
help, delegating. You don't have to have all the answers,
you don't have to work it all out by yourself. Asking for
help can be liberating. The right help at the right time
can be the difference between success and failure.

*The Expert – Experts measure their competence based on
'what' and 'how much' they know or can do. Believing*

they will never know enough, they fear being exposed as inexperienced or lacking knowledge.

Being an expert, being the authority, is an important part of success. It's about having the confidence that you can deliver what you say you are going to deliver. If you are clear on who you are, how you add value, and transparent in how you go about your work, then why shouldn't you feel confident about it? You don't need a certificate to prove things. You need action. If you are hiding behind 'the expert' and procrastinating because you can't do something until you get more skills, then we are here to call you out. Put the course down, come out from behind the certificate and get on with it.

Tackling imposter syndrome

Imposter syndrome is a way of telling you to be kinder to yourself, and, in doing so, kinder to others. You can use your wobbles, your doubts, your blockers to inspire others. When you share how you really feel, people connect with you, understand you better and empathize.

The next time you start to feel you are getting in your way, think about what is driving your behaviour. If you can't move on yourself, get help. Don't let imposter syndrome shackle you.

CASE STUDY – Max

'I joined my previous employer straight from college and over my nineteen years I moved up through the ranks. I loved it! I worked with some fantastic people and for some great managers who took an interest in my development. During this period, my partner and I had three children, we moved house a number of times and generally loved life.

'Then I learned that my role was "at risk" and that I would have to apply for one of the new roles in the new organization. So after nineteen years I left the business.

'I used the consultation period to start job searches, update my CV, update LinkedIn and generally reach out to a few of my network, including recruitment agencies. The gardening leave and non-working period was quite simply one of the best periods of my life. It was a beautiful summer; the dog has never been walked as much and I finally made a dent in the long list of DIY tasks that had been building up over the last year. However, I was concerned about what the future held.

'The early work I had put in on my job search and CV started to pay off. I had a number of interviews lined up, which was a big relief as much of my concern had been about whether anyone would want me after nineteen years in one place. I kept myself busy between interviews. I spoiled the family with a few treats, had the garden done and tried to keep fit. I had a decision to make about the route I would prefer to take my career. I had dabbled with starting my own consultancy business. I started to look at well-paid short-term contract work. But eventually I decided to continue to focus on permanent employment.

'Redundancy can knock you for six, but remember what you are worth. One great bit of advice I had was regarding interviews: "It's not just about you impressing them, they need to impress you too." This statement was very true. I actually turned down a better-paid job, closer to home, in preference to my current role for exactly this reason.

'Remember your support group. There were a number of us affected; some stayed, some didn't, but the support we gave each other was great. The P45 Gang WhatsApp group is still alive and kicking and the home of nostalgic banter.'

Bouncebackability

You will have setbacks and failures and 'Noes', and small victories and glorious 'Yeses'. You know when the answer was 42 in *The Hitchhiker's Guide to the Galaxy*, but no one knew what it meant? Well, it means how many times you will get a no before you get a yes . . . forty-two. So how are you going to handle forty-two 'Noes'? Dealing with rejection will teach you so much about the sort of person you are. It is worth working on how we respond to set-backs, and training ourselves to improve our response to build our resilience.

What should our resilience-training schedule look like?

Take control of your thoughts. Is life happening to you, or are you creating life? When life happens to you, exercise your right to choose the option that benefits you the most.

- Work on your 'what ifs'. When something happens to you, do you instantly worry? Is your mind full of negative 'what ifs' or positive curiosity? Experts say that on average we have 60,000 thoughts per day. Of those, 95 per cent repeat each day and, on average, 80 per cent of repeated ideas are negative. Our 'what ifs' are mostly negative. However, what if our 'what ifs' become mostly positive? Imagine that. In Amber Rae's book *Choose Wonder Over Worry*, she wonders about possibilities, opportunities, time to think. The skill of 'wonder over worry' is known as cognitive agility. Cognitive agility is the art and science of knowing that you can choose whether to operate in default mode (which might be negative and defensive) or adjust to make better choices. Next time you worry, be more curious about what you are worrying about. Is it real? Is there an alternative? Can you choose just to let go of the worry?

- Treat failure as just one step closer to success. Resilient people treat problems as a learning process. We have talked about stepping out of your comfort zone and into stretch. In your stretch zone, you need to be prepared to fail as part of the process. When you learn from mistakes you get closer to your goals. Every time you say, 'Well, I won't do that again,' you are building your resilience and strengthening your response towards a more positive outcome.

- Train yourself to enjoy the stretch zone, and not fear the stress zone. What lengths do you go to to avoid perceived discomfort? If you have ever tried yoga you can relate to the feeling of being

'The difference between winners and losers is not whether they face obstacles and setbacks – we all do, it is inevitable things don't go to plan, that events surprise us, mistakes happen. The real difference is that "winners" bounce back from a fumble by refusing to panic, analysing the situation, and looking for positive action so they can correct the problem.'

Rosabeth Moss Kanter

twisted into a pose that is, at first, very uncomfortable. However, when you lean into the pose, breathe into it rather than resist it, a sense of stillness and calm happens. If you let yourself enter your stretch zone, it will feel more comfortable over time. The training isn't about avoiding stretch, it's about embracing it. And if stretch turns into stress, you do the same. Lean into it. Think about the cause of the thoughts and tension and think about what you can learn about it. If you fear the stress zone so much, you may end up creating it. Rethink how you feel about what is happening to you. Observe how your body and mind feel and adjust how you are thinking about it. If you feel like shouting out 'Why me?' then that is the moment to think 'What next?' instead . . . begin to think about your 'other door'.

Use your priority list to keep you motivated when the tug of war gets tough. The final exercise on the training schedule is something we've already been working on: purpose. Your priority list. Resilient people have a clear sense of purpose that enables them to stay in the game even when things get tough. It is much harder to feel defeated when what you're working towards has a deep sense of meaning for you.

Resilience is many things to many people. However, resilience is not, ever, stiff upper lip, carry on regardless, show no emotion, admit no hurt. You can't function like that. Your inner world will eventually implode.

Training yourself to be more resilient will take time. However, if you keep going, instead of feeling like you are constantly getting knocked down and having to get up again, you will see it will take more to knock you down in the first place. That's not to say we are training to become completely non-responsive, it's about responding in a positive way, so when you have to dig in, and pull the rope, the tug of war is pulled over the positive line.

Break Time!

When things are not going very well it is important to take time to recharge. It is not stopping – it's taking a break, stepping back and returning ready to fire on all cylinders. If you can elevate yourself just above the noise and find calm in that space, you gain perspective that will give you the energy to keep going. And have a positive impact. Sometimes our emotions get in the way of seeing the bigger picture so taking some time out gives you space to gather yourself, recharge and go again.

What Do You Do if You are Not in Control?
Take a big deep breath, make your belly
expand. Breathe out. And repeat.

Like leaves falling from the tree, and blowing
away in the wind, just let go for a few moments.
Float above it all.

If you are doing all you can, trying everything
you can, taking all opportunities, and things still
aren't shifting then take some time to step back.
You can only do your best. No one is expecting
anything more.

A key part of being resilient is knowing when it is
time to step out.

It is not giving up or quitting but staying in place
and breathing. It's about taking the pressure off
for a while so that you can return with more
perspective and energy.

Get Creative

You might not think of yourself as creative but creativity is thinking of ideas, of solutions, of what ifs. Everyone is creative.

We all need to be creative to survive.

Creativity can be rearranging the living room to be cosier.

It can be making a meal by following a recipe.

It can be inventing something that changes the world.

Being creative can be small and it can be large.

We *all* have the power to be creative.

What stops us is our notion of having to have all the answers straight away, of having to be an expert straight away, of getting everything right straight away.

So we say we aren't creative.

What really stops you from drawing, from painting, from making stuff? No interest? Or thinking that you are no good at it?

So give it a go now. Get some paper and draw something. Anything.

What is the difference between what you have just drawn and some abstract modern art? Yes, technically quite a lot, but the lesson is that an artist believes they are an artist *before* they start to create. Therefore, they create with intention. They accept mistakes are part of it. They accept they do not have all the answers.

'Creativity is mistakes.'

Grayson Perry

Be more artist

Use your creativity and imagination to help you solve problems as they come your way. You do not have to have all the answers right now to how you are going to do something.

You do not need to know how you are going to get your perfect job, launch your business idea, start something new.

You do have to make the first move.

You do have to be open to try things.

You do have to know you might fail.

You do have to believe that anything is possible.

Being Curious

I got curious about starting a blog. I watched a webinar. I started a blog. I joined a local network event. There was a talk about writing a book. I went to a workshop. I met some people. They recommended a Facebook group. I saw a Facebook ad for a book-coaching programme. I signed up. I met my book agent. And here is the book. And I am still following breadcrumbs to see what's next.

OK, it wasn't quite like that. In between were a lot of tries, fails, wins, struggles and over-optimism. Rejection and feeling like a failure played heavily. Giving up was a regular temptation. But the curiosity stayed around, it lingered and it meant I carried on. What else could I do?

Being curious is about opening up to everything around you. Seeing opportunities, experiencing new things, meeting new people. It is just opening up, without having an expected outcome.

Do something today just because you are curious

- Listen to a podcast (search podcast/curious).
- Read a book (go into a charity shop, go to the book section, see what jumps out).

- Watch a TED talk (the first one you find in your search).
- Go to a network event (check out the Meet Up app and see what's on in your area).
- Speak to three strangers (be curious about them).

'Follow the breadcrumbs. You never know where they lead. New people, new places, new opportunities.'

Amanda Paradine, career coach

Let Go of Judgement

Judging yourself, and judging others, holds you back.

Stop going to judgemental groups

Groupthink is everywhere in our life. It's the parent groups that meet to talk about how bad the teachers are – is this contributing to a solution, or is it social bullying? The sports club that meets and the main topic is the state of the facilities – are you talking solutions, or apportioning blame? Think about the group of people you talk to about losing your job. About how bad the business is; about what is going wrong back in the office. It might feel like a support network, but question how much those conversations are helping you move forward. Beware that sometimes your tribe may be the very thing that is holding you back.

Stop judging others, and yourself

Seeing all that is wrong with others, and spending time judging them, is not helping you. And the worst kind of judgement is that of yourself. Judgement can consume a lot of energy, so it is never helpful.

Suspend your judgement while you try new things.

Instead of judgement, try kindness

If someone asks for help, or asks for your opinion, try kindness not judgement. If you feel yourself putting pressure on yourself, try being kind. Be kind to yourself.

Stay in Your Lane

If you are about to throw yourself, all in, into a new world, stand by for action. There are many things ready to keep you in your place or send you off in a different direction. Your mind might be the first adversary, as it begins to tell you stories and find excuses why things will not happen. Your friends and family might create another battle. Getting the wrong advice, or the right advice but at the wrong time, might get you into a third battle.

You will start to get messages from experts:

- 'Stop trading your time for money.'
- 'Start to reduce time you spend on your businesses.'
- 'Work hard and you'll get results.'
- 'Stop giving away all your secrets.'
- 'Start giving away all your secrets.'

There is so much noise out there. That is all it is. Noise. Turn it down. You might be signing up to lots of 'stuff'. Trying to get help to propel you forward. You will get on email lists and social-media feeds. All of these messages, whether emails, webinars, social media – are marketing headlines. Yes, they may be able to help you. But own your plan. Find the help you need. Not the help you think you might need because someone has a great marketing campaign. Do not get sidetracked.

Spend time thinking about what you need, what your gaps are, how you want this to work – and then go out and find people who will help fill those gaps. Stay in your lane. It is good to follow people who are doing similar things to those you want to do. If they are active on social media or have a blog it's great learning and inspiration. However, it is exactly that, it is there to help. The noise might turn to despair, as you start to feel you'll never be that good, that successful. If things start to feel like they aren't helping, turn them off.

Your Next Door

When a door closes in your life it is easy to think of the past and everything you are losing. But as you let go and start to look to the future and the possibilities you will see that you have nothing to lose by embracing this gifted opportunity.

CASE STUDY – Dan

'When I was made redundant I didn't really understand the journey or how rough the road to recovery would get or be. I was never one for throwing in the towel or admitting defeat but at times it was difficult to manage and keep a lid on things. Reflecting back, it was the kick up the ass I needed as opportunities often arise when you are least expecting them.

'After I was made redundant I went straight out and started to look for work, I wanted to work in a different field and took a £50k salary reduction to get a foot in the door. There was huge financial pressure and keeping on top of our household commitments was my priority.

'I decided to explore upskilling by starting a diploma in health and safety in order to be more employable and attractive to businesses. It was a balancing act but I knew I really wanted to be in that field.

'Reflecting on our experience of redundancy it was the best thing that happened to us as a family. We are now in a position where we have adjusted our outgoings and learned from it all.

'I had my wife behind me, pushing me forward, encouraging me, and helping me to "dig in" – the words she used on more than one occasion. You need a supporting element to succeed and positive people, not the doom and gloomers.

'Sometimes life serves up a menu that does not really take your fancy but you soon realize to eat what is in front of you and use it as fuel. One thing for sure, it is about believing in yourself, using the energy of others to motivate yourself when times are tough. It is easy when the conditions are favourable but when life is against you it is how you apply yourself.'

Building for Tomorrow

When you start something new it is so easy to get lost, very quickly, in the comparison alley. You feel like you should be an equal to people in your space immediately. Then you quickly start telling yourself that you are not in that space, you are not as good, and you find reasons and facts to back up your story. If you are starting out with a fresh mission – to get a bigger job, to go freelance, to start a business – you need to remind yourself of your long-term plan every day. And it *is* a long-term plan. You are not building for the now, you are creating your future.

You have to enjoy your now and know that it's building tomorrow. You cannot wish, or worry, your days away. If you are not enjoying your day today, you need to work on how you are going to change that.

Do not live in the 'once X happens it will be all right'. 'Once I get a job, once I get the first client, once I get my logo . . .' Once all that happens, there will be something else for you to shift your worry to. That is what all the YouTubers and Instagrammers and bloggers mean when they say 'Just start'. Those dreaded words that I used to hear when I was going to start-up conferences and watching webinars. The message isn't 'Just dive into any old thing', the message is 'Start doing things now that will help you get somewhere else in the future. Hold your nerve.'

It took me twelve months of swishing about, lost. I wish I had written this chapter beforehand so I could have read it. I worried every day, precious days that I could've been reading, walking, talking to new people, attending events, getting out here. There is a reason why you bought this book. You want things to change. You know there is more to life. You have more to give. What you start doing now creates your tomorrow.

If You are Finding It Hard to Move On

Listen to yourself, know where you are. If you begin to feel hopeless for a long period, you might need to look for extra support. Losing your job can be a positive thing, but the initial shock can be hard. It is a time of change, loneliness, uncertainty, and it can understandably get too much.

When to seek counselling

Counselling can help you identify how and why you are in the situation you are in, and to think about changing that situation if you want to (you have to want to change). Counselling can involve talking about early life experiences including childhood and linking back to current issues. Counselling is a less intense form of psychotherapy. It can be difficult to admit you need help, but counselling could be the start of a transformational time for you.

Counselling might benefit you:

- If something is troubling you and you are having difficulty finding a solution on your own.
- If things feel overwhelming, are getting on top of you, and you don't feel you can move on.
- If things are having a negative impact on your work and/or relationships.

- If you're finding it hard to talk to friends and family.
- If you're feeling anxious.
- If you feel you may be depressed.

Have a look on www.mind.org.uk. It will help you through your feelings.

Own It

If you have been in corporate life for a while, you may have gone through a phase of feeling frustrated because you cannot just get on and do stuff. You felt held back, you felt unheard. Well, if ever there was a time to feel completely empowered, completely enabled to just get on and do stuff it's now. With no bosses, peers or stakeholders to keep you in your place you now only have yourself to wrestle with.

You have more power than you might think. It's time to own it. The most empowered you have ever been. Own whatever you really want to do, take responsibility, take actions and take the glory when it all works out.

So, What are You Going to Do?

We are here. You are here.

It's nearly the end (of the book).

Haven't we been on a journey?

Well done for getting to this point.

We've been through the shock, the feeling of being stuck, the feeling of slowing down to get clarity, the feeling of becoming unstuck and now we are thriving! Aren't we?

If you've been making notes throughout the read, then now is the time to go back.

Where were you?

Where are you now?

Have you been keeping hope alive?

Where have your ideas taken you? How have they evolved?

What action have you taken already? Is there anything that surprises you?

You know you are going to make changes. How big will they be?

Are you sticking, twisting or busting out?

Top tip to thrive

If you do just one thing now write down – in big words – your ideal tomorrow scenario. If it all were to come together and your ideal scenario were to exist tomorrow – what would it look like? OK the intention is set. You are on your way.

Wherever you are going next, remember that you are in control, it's all there for you to take.

You've got this.

Own it.

You aren't alone.

Keep your hope a force for change, keep your ideas coming to solve problems, and keep taking action.

You are about to make losing your job the best thing that has ever happened to you.

Resources

Part 1 – Shock

Martin Lewis's MoneySavingExpert website has a huge range of suggestions to reduce monthly outgoings: www.moneysavingexpert.com.

There are several charities and organizations which offer free help, advice and legal support to those facing redundancy such as Citizens Advice (www.citizensadvice.org.uk), The Advisory, Conciliation and Arbitration Service (ACAS) (www.acas.org.uk), Step Change (www.stepchange.org), Turn2Us (www.turn2us.org.uk), Pregnant Then Screwed (https://pregnantthenscrewed.com/), Money Advice Service (www.moneyadviceservice.org.uk/) and many more depending on your location.

Todd Kashdan and Robert Biswas-Diener, *The Upside of Your Dark Side: Why Being Your Whole Self – Not Just Your 'Good' Self – Drives Success and Fulfillment* (Plume, 2015).

Part 2 – Stuck

Paul McGee, *S.U.M.O. (Shut Up, Move On): The Straight-Talking Guide to Succeeding in Life* (Capstone, 2015).

Bill Burnett and Dave Evans, *Designing Your Life: How to Build a Well-Lived, Joyful Life* (Penguin, 2016).

Cal Newport, *Digital Minimalism: Choosing a Focused Life in a Noisy World* (Portfolio Penguin, 2019).

Part 3 – Slow, Slow, Go

Simon Sinek, *Start with Why: How Great Leaders Inspire Everyone to Take Action* (Portfolio, 2011).

Helen Tupper and Sarah Ellis, *The Squiggly Career: Ditch the Ladder, Discover Opportunity, Design Your Career* (Portfolio Penguin, 2020).

Karen Barrow et al., *Smarter Living: Work Nest Invest Relate Thrive* (Black Dog & Leventhal, 2020).

Stephen R. Covey, *The 7 Habits of Highly Effective People: Powerful Lessons in Personal Change* (Franklin Covey on Brilliance Audio, 2012).

Dietary advice: mind.org.uk/food; freelancedietitian. org; bant.org.uk.

Part 4 – Unstuck

James Reed, *The 7-Second CV: How to Land the Interview* (Virgin Books, 2019).

Leapers freelance support network with Matthew Knight: www.leapers.co.

Emma Gannon, *The Multi-Hyphen Method: Work Less, Create More, and Design a Career That Works for You* (Hodder, 2019).

The Happy Startup School learning community of entrepreneurs: www.thehappystartupschool.com.

Jessica Killingley's Rockstar Writers Academy: www. rockstarwritersacademy.com.

Part 5 – Thrive

Carol Dweck, *Mindset: Changing the Way You Think to Fulfil Your Potential* (Ballantine Books, 2007).

Susan Jeffers, *Feel the Fear and Do It Anyway: How to Turn Your Fear and Indecision into Confidence and Action* (Vermilion, 2007).

Amber Rae, *Choose Wonder Over Worry: Move Beyond Fear and Doubt to Unlock Your Full Potential* (Piatkus, 2018).

For advice and support on mental health: www.mind.org.uk.

Acknowledgements

Thank you to all the breadcrumbs who were involved in the making and creating of this book. It all started . . . well where, where did it start? Maybe at the DO Lectures, maybe at a workshop with Robin Waite, my first business coach, maybe while drinking coffee with Helen Hodgkinson, maybe while chatting to Louise Mitchell (my redundancy buddies), maybe while on a call to Debbie, Fiona, Laura, Lorainne, Stef, Esther, Jo, Julie, Jade, Nicola, Annie, Louise, Jacque, Pedro, Bonita, Danny, Jason. Maybe it's thank you to the business that made me redundant? From there the breadcrumbs grew and many people played a part to shift me along: Ruth Kudzi, the Happy Startups Laurence and Carlos, the Woodborough Entrepreneurs, Alison and Martin Grady, Tracey McEachran, Helen Chapman (who all popped into my life when I needed a boost during gardening leave).

Phil, Jo, Susan, Vicky, Ceri, Keith, Martin and Dan, who were the first members and part of creating the Another Door community, and who read the very first draft of the book.

And then Jessica Killingley. I sat in a cupboard at the business centre in Portsmouth as she talked Elisabeth and me through how to write a book. She was my coach, and now my agent.

And then family of course. My husband, my mum, my

dad, my brother, my daughter, who all quietly tolerate my random ideas, my energy to do stuff (often at 3 a.m., where this book started), my low days when things don't go to plan. I have an amazing family and friends network, they are my energy, and my why. I could not have done this without Martina, Celia and the team at Penguin. Thank you so much for getting 'it' and helping me grow the seed into a flower. You have made this small idea a big dream.

And thank you to you for reading this book.

It's pointless writing a book if no one reads it.

So thank you for being a part of it too. And I'm excited to be part of what happens to your next chapter and door opening.

PENGUIN PARTNERSHIPS

Penguin Partnerships is the Creative Sales and Promotions team at Penguin Random House. We have a long history of working with clients on a wide variety of briefs, specializing in brand promotions, bespoke publishing and retail exclusives, plus corporate, entertainment and media partnerships.

We can respond quickly to briefs and specialize in repurposing books and content for sales promotions, for use as incentives and retail exclusives as well as creating content for new books in collaboration with our partners as part of branded book relationships.

Equally if you'd simply like to buy a bulk quantity of one of our existing books at a special discount, we can help with that too. Our books can make excellent corporate or employee gifts.

Special editions, including personalized covers, excerpts of existing books or books with corporate logos can be created in large quantities for special needs.

We can work within your budget to deliver whatever you want, however you want it.

For more information, please contact
salesenquiries@penguinrandomhouse.co.uk